WHAT TO DO
BETWEEN
BIRTH AND DEATH

WHAT TO DO BETWEEN BIRTH AND DEATH

The Art of Growing Up

CHARLES SPEZZANO, PH.D.

WILLIAM MORROW AND COMPANY, INC.
New York

It is the policy of William Morrow and Company, Inc., and its imprints and affiliates, recognizing the importance of preserving what has been written, to print the books we publish on acid-free paper, and we exert our best efforts to that end.

Library of Congress Cataloging-in-Publication Data

Spezzano, Charles.
    What to do between birth and death : the art of growing up /
Charles Spezzano.
        p.   cm.
    ISBN 0-688-10399-5
    1. Self-actualization (Psychology)   I. Title.
BF637.S4S684   1992
158—dc20   91-20737
                                                                              CIP

Printed in the United States of America

First Edition

1   2   3   4   5   6   7   8   9   10

BOOK DESIGN BY PAUL CHEVANNES

For Jill, Keri, Brooke,
and Spencer

Contents

CONTENTS

Introduction

Most people over twenty-one look like grown-ups—at least from the outside.

Most people over twenty-one feel like teenagers inside.

This confuses a lot of people. The mirror tells them one thing, their emotions tell them another, and a third little voice inside scolds, "A grown-up would know how to handle this situation."

That little voice often directs people into my office, and says, "You're the expert, tell me what to do."

And I am the expert. Sort of. I've got the graduate degrees, I've got the fifty-pound texts on my shelves. I've listened to hundreds of patients, many of whom consider themselves to be more satisfied with their lives since our sessions. But still, this therapy business is an odd profession in many ways. I'm being paid not to share the wealth and breadth of my knowledge about human nature, but to listen closely and offer insights into the specific problems of each person who walks into my office.

Most of my patients are distressed not just by having a particular problem with a mate, a child, a job, a parent, but also by the fact that they're so perplexed about how to handle the problem. Surely, they think, others see life clearly, with a blinding clarity that they don't.

You know what? They're right. Some people—not many, but enough for most of us to know at least one or two—are grown-ups both inside and out. It's not that they're without problems, but they have a seemingly instinctive understanding and sense of reality about life's curveballs. Their careers, their personal lives, and their interior lives are all moving forward. And for them this book would be nothing more than a review of how adulthood works. They already know that life is an experiment, that marriage is a process, that careers change, that friendships are based on power as well as affection, that parenthood has to be invented anew for each child, and why certain people and situations make them feel uncomfortable. Is it instinct, good parenting, an insightful analysis, or perfect genes that's given them this ready understanding of adulthood? And if that question can't be answered, can we at least take what they know, distill it, and pass around the bottle of knowledge so the rest of us—who don't feel like "total" adults inside—can finish growing up?

Well, that's what I've tried to do here. Share this common-sense wisdom with you. I'll be talking a lot about this sense of being a genuine grown-up and the wisdom on which it is based—what it feels like inside—throughout the book. The process of writing down my ideas about this has clarified a lot for me. Sharing these essays with my family and friends has toughened me up a bit, and for that I am indebted to them. I hope these chapters spark discussions and reappraisals, and bring your internal and external pictures a little bit closer together.

PART ONE

How Adulthood Works

Adulthood: The Experiment

Moving into a new university office about ten years ago, I found two items left behind in a desk drawer by the previous occupant: a Spalding rubber ball and a cassette tape on which was recorded a lecture given by Joseph Campbell to a group of students. One of the gems of that lecture was this remark: "The first fact about the human being as an animal is that he is born twelve years too soon."

We spend the first twelve years of our life dependent on others, and we worry constantly what they will think and say about what we do. This attitude becomes firmly rooted in our psyches during those twelve years. "What will Mother say? What will Daddy say? Who will help me now? What should I do?" Then we hit adolescence, and the "big people" start to expect that we will be something they call responsible; that is, they expect that having been parented for twelve years, we have learned how to parent ourselves.

Unfortunately for most of us, that's no more likely than any of us hitting a baseball like Ken Griffey, Jr., or a tennis ball like Steffi Graf just because we watch a lot of major-league games or Wimbledon matches. Learning involves doing as well as observing, but we really don't teach our children to parent themselves during their first twelve years. We just parent them, and that's different. It leaves them, as it left us, ready to be parented. Only in a very limited way does it set in motion the process of learning to parent oneself.

The neurotic is understood by most therapists, despite their disagreements about other issues, to be someone who never crosses over from childhood dependency into adult self-management. In business for themselves, as we all are, neurotics keep hoping for a takeover and will often settle for a hostile one if nothing better comes along. They unconsciously believe they will be safer if someone who knows how to run a life is in charge of theirs. They figure that there must be real adults, but they are not among them.

I say "they," but that's self-protective. We all struggle to maintain a foothold in our own adulthoods—to keep ourselves from giving the momentum in our lives away to a real other person or to a parental image inside our heads. And at times we all fail in this effort. Helping adolescents make a solid transition from childhood to adulthood is not one of the strong points of our society. So we all slip back.

Some of the big people we knew as children are carried around inside us, and we keep trying to get them—and any of our peers who we assume are real adults when we aren't feeling that way about ourselves—to tell us what we should be doing. It seems impossible to us that our only guidelines will be those vague urges and ambitions we experience inside ourselves. There must be a way to figure out what to do, with the same kind of reassuring certainty we felt when our big parents told their little children what to do. But there isn't.

That's it. That's what Campbell was suggesting. And it's the first key principle of adulthood. *You make it up.* You make up your adulthood. The only clues are those images and urges and "maybes" that float in front of your mind's eye. No one else can be of any help in sorting it out. You do what you want, and then you see what happens. The talking it over with friends—with its implication of "What do you think about what I want to do, where I want to live, who I want to marry, how I want to work"—is just a last-ditch attempt to avoid that moment when you say, "I'm doing . . ." Any predesigned scheme is someone else's game plan, to which, if you take the advice too seriously, you voluntarily submit. As William Blake said, "I must create a system or be enslaved by another man's." There is no third choice.

That makes your life an experiment. Like an experimenter, you do want to know what other experimenters have found out. But at some point, you have to say, *what if?* Otherwise, it's not an experiment, just a repetition. And because it's an experiment, you're not supposed to know exactly how it will turn out. If it always turns out the way you think it will, you're doing something wrong. So after you ask what if, you just do it, and then you know for yourself.

Sure, there are some things that people have tried often enough, with bad results, so that you might be expected to know ahead of time how things will turn out if you try to do them. You probably shouldn't invade Russia in the wintertime or start a land war in Southeast Asia; and there are philosophical and ethical arguments that have already been written down that should convince you that murdering and exploiting others doesn't contribute to the kind of world where anyone ends up feeling good. But maybe you should start a magazine or restaurant even though most of them fail. What you really want is to know ahead of time how it will turn out, so you don't have to get hurt in the experiment. Life doesn't work that way. It used to, when you were a child, but it doesn't anymore.

Whenever I see people in therapy struggle with whether to stay with their current lover or career, they always start out with the unspoken wish to know how life will be five years from now if they stay or go, quit or keep working. They are waiting to find that out before they decide. Of course, if they knew that, then the decision would become a nondecision. Decisions mean doing it when you don't know.

I've come to believe that I should be telling my kids more often than I do that I don't know. I don't know how things will turn out for them if they try this or that. Most of the time I can only say, "If you decide to do this or that, I'll help if I can." What they really need practice at is making decisions, and we so rarely have the patience and the tolerance for the pain we feel when seeing them fall on their face to give them that chance.

Doing What You Say
You'll Do

Most detective-novel fans look forward to the hard-boiled wisdom dropped in bits and pieces by the hero during the story.
My favorite is one from Robert Parker, creator of the Spenser
series. One of Spenser's prime criteria for evaluating people is
whether or not they do what they say they'll do. For him it's
a moral issue. For me it's practical. Life gets very complicated
when we say we'll do things and then don't.

Most of us sense that this is not a great way to operate. But
the usual solution we come up with is to bend ourselves into
pretzels trying to fulfill whatever commitment we made. An
alternative that seems to work much more smoothly in the
lives of the few people I've seen use it is not to make too many
commitments—or, put another way, to keep quiet as long as
possible in the face of other people's needs.

That has a callous edge to it, but it works for everyone
concerned. We all need something or other all the time. And

we all have ways of communicating those needs to people around us. Sometimes we just say directly what we need. Often we get it across through nonverbal emotional channels. However the transmission takes place, the key moment is when we realize that someone around us needs something. It is very difficult to stifle the reflexive "I'll help," or the soon-to-be-forgotten "There might be something I can do to help," or the infamous "I think I can help you with that."

Check it out first. When you are ready to help, just do it. When you are ready to invite someone over for dinner, invite him. Don't tell him you'd like to have him over sometime. If you'd like it, what's stopping you from inviting him now? Promises are useless preludes to real action. Children make promises all the time. Childhood is a time of potential. Adulthood is the time for doing what you can and not talking about what you can't.

How Not to Explain or
Justify Yourself

At a dinner recently a friend of mine was asked by another guest what she did for a living. It happens that she teaches breathing techniques. This is a form of therapy often associated with "rebirthers." Some people find rebirthers hokey because some of them have claimed that their therapies actually—not just symbolically—take people through the traumas of their birth experiences and repair the distress left over from such early events. The guest apparently made an association between teaching breathing techniques and rebirthing, and, although many nonrebirther therapists now incorporate either the teaching of breathing or at least the monitoring of changes in breathing into their approach to patients, once he mentally classified all breath work as a subcategory of rebirthing, he seemed to experience the same feeling of moral outrage about breathing as he obviously does about rebirthing. So he began to grill this person whom he had just met, essentially demanding, through a series of questions, that she justify her practicing a method of therapy to which he objected.

Unfortunately, she tried to answer each question as if she were only being asked for information that would help him clarify his understanding of her work. As she became what she felt was more cooperative, he read "cooperative" as "submissive." So—as always happens in sadomasochistic encounters like this—he became more hostile, and she found herself increasingly backed into a corner.

Whenever I think of that transaction, I wish she had said, "I feel that you're asking me to justify my work. I don't want to do that right now. Maybe we could find something else to talk about." It is so easy to start answering the most unreasonable questions, as if some adult with legitimate authority were asking the child in us to explain himself or herself. When a question makes you uncomfortable, it's worth stopping to consider that it's a lousy question and it's not that you don't have a good answer.

What Experts Know

If you're in financial trouble, your lawyer doesn't know *if* you should declare bankruptcy. Lawyers only know how to file bankruptcies. They don't know who *should* do it. When you ask a lawyer if you should declare bankruptcy, you're asking her if she thinks you should hire her and pay her money—if she thinks you should buy what she sells. It's the same if you ask an attorney if you should sue somebody. In an awful lot of instances he will say yes, you should. You should, that is, buy the service he sells.

This is not a diatribe against lawyers. The same applies to me and my colleagues. Psychotherapists don't know if you should be in analysis or some other form of psychotherapy. We only know how to help you do it if that's what you want to do. We rarely tell people that they don't need or wouldn't benefit from some sort of psychological treatment, just as chiropractors usually believe that only through a couple of years of their guidance and service will you be able to restructure your chronic underlying skeletal distortions and damages, and just as periodontists—professionals who, by definition, think that the good life starts with great gums—believe that everyone over thirty needs gum surgery.

The wish for an authority with *all* the answers we need to run our lives is a powerful universal fantasy. I have seen several older men I loved turn themselves over passively to medical-care systems that may well have made the wrong decisions for them. No amount of support from family members would persuade them to challenge their physicians even to the extent of asking for another opinion from outside that hospital where they eventually died. Women have derived some strength in this respect from the feminist literature about the shortcomings of a male medical system in understanding their health needs, but that's just one aspect of this broader problem of sorting out in what ways certain experts are smarter than we are and in what ways they cannot be. Our own desire that they be omniscient keeps us from seeing the limits of their expertise.

How Adulthood Reaches
Critical Mass

When I've seen patients move during the course of therapy from psychological adolescence to adulthood, it has always involved a cyclical repetition of these steps: access to a new piece of wisdom about how adulthood works, individualizing this wisdom into a specific wish for change in their life, deciding to act in some new way, and taking action. This happens over and over. At some point the combination of wisdom and practice making things happen reaches critical mass, and we're there—adulthood.

When I listened to Bill Moyers interview Joseph Campbell, I thought Campbell revealed his own transition into adulthood. Even though he didn't label it that way, it was a good example of the point I'm making. He quit graduate school and went off to read mythology and anything else that intrigued him, because that's what he wanted to do.

He never got his Ph.D. and never became Dr. Campbell.

Instead, he just read and wrote about and taught mythology. He didn't want to do whatever else *they* wanted him to do to become Dr. Campbell.

I don't believe that you have to quit something to become an adult, or that quitting in the middle of a professional training program necessarily means you've made the transition. There does, however, have to be a moment of consequence when you say yes or no completely on your own authority.

When Campbell went to the woods to read a broad range of books that spoke to him rather than stay locked within a narrow academic curriculum prescribed by his faculty, his adulthood reached critical mass. As Moyers put it, he was saying "The hell with it!" The "it" here is external authority that has no legal or moral binding force in our lives but to which we submit out of habit or fear.

We all know when life presents us with the opportunity to say the hell with it. Either we say it or we don't. Each time any of us says it in a situation of consequence, that brings our adulthood closer to critical mass. It's saying that you will move forward by taking your own best guess at the right direction.

A patient of mine told me bits and pieces of the story of a woman named Deborah Meier who was a friend of his family and about whom I have since read stories in a few places. She was one of many teachers who feel trapped and hopeless in the massive and largely unsuccessful two-hundred-year-old public-school system. Her saying the hell with it took the form of opening a school in East Harlem, the incredible success of which led to her eventually winning a MacArthur Foundation Fellowship.

But I was equally impressed by the parents of a psychotic boy who would have been institutionalized if they hadn't said the hell with professional opinion and corporate inability to respond to individual circumstances. They learned furniture repair together and created a business in their home so they could take care of their son. I don't know how successful they were in keeping him out of permanent confinement, but they saw their dilemma as their own unique problem, and accepted their subjective experience of their situation as something no one else could view exactly that way. With a conviction in the wisdom of that perspective, they created a new vision of what their lives might be that included a reasonable income and their son, and they acted on it.

There is no magic in that story. During one session I said to them that their unspoken wish to have someone come up with a new and creative solution to their problem was not going to be realized. There were only the options all the other professionals they had consulted had already told them about and whatever they could come up with on their own. They didn't open a school for psychotic children like the one Deborah Meier opened for children in Harlem. They just took care of their own needs in a way that fit them. To do that, they had to accept that no one else had any motive to create a new system to suit their specific blends of needs and wishes. Once that piece of wisdom took root, they recognized that their choices were either to use the options out there or make up a new one. No less courageously or creatively than Campbell or Meier, they created their own version of adulthood.

Good Luck and Bad Luck

If you want to understand anyone at a certain moment, there is perhaps nothing more essential you could know about him than whether he experiences what psychologists call *the locus of control* in his life to be inside of him or in the hands of someone else. The concept of locus of control is one of the most robust in psychology, and also one of the most straightforward.

All of us experience ourselves as both active and reactive. We act willfully, but we also react to what the world presents to us. The critical question is whether we believe that the scale is tipped in the direction of us being in control of our behavior or on the side of external forces determining what we do. That's locus of control.

You cannot have a real adult problem-solving approach to life unless you feel empowered, and what empowers us is a sense of an internal locus of control—I can make things happen. But there is also validity to the position taken by Rabbi Kushner in When Bad Things Happen to Good People: Things happen to us; we do not control the universe.

Existentialist therapists say we should look at adulthood as something we create. Deterministic therapists encourage us to accept that sometimes bad things happen. I think we carry versions of these two therapists in our minds, and we consult whichever one suits our purposes at particular moments. This can lead to some contradictory interesting attitudes. For some, good outcomes are always due to our virtues and bad outcomes to rotten luck. And for others, it works the other way around. All the lousy stuff is our fault, and all the good happenings are luck. Or our good fortune took hard work and everyone else's was due to their being "lucky bastards." And a very popular variation is to view everyone else's misfortune as due to their incompetence and lousy judgment. That way we don't have to worry that a similar bad thing can happen to us. All we have to do is avoid the other guy's stupidity, and we're immune to those bad things that happened to him.

There is a natural wisdom in this apparent craziness: "locus of control" is just a fancy way to talk about luck and responsibility as the two basic explanations for why life is working out the way it is. And it's clear that while we can't totally control life, we can get very good at switching back and forth between attributing events in our lives to luck or taking responsibility for them.

If you can do it with self-awareness and humor, you can ease the burden of not always knowing how life works. We should all know about balancing our senses of luck and responsibility, which you can call, if you want to sound psychologically sophisticated, locus-of-control management. We should be taught it in school, maybe get yellow and brown and black belts in its management, like the ones karate schools award for increasing degrees of skill. The coveted ninth-degree black belts will be awarded to those of us who are so good at switching between luck and responsibility to explain why things happen to us that we can feel helpless whenever that attitude maintains our self-esteem (ironic, but a good dose of helplessness in the face of a major screw-up can be a real lifesaver to our self-esteem), and then can turn around in the blink of an eye and experience ourselves as completely self-directed when that suits our purposes (Hey, I don't have to take this; I'm out of here!).

Yes, I think that should be a course taught from first grade through college: locus-of-control management. We do it all the time anyway. We might as well do it well.

Human Containers

People that we experience as genuine adults, as having character and maturity—"having their shit together," as we have come to put it—are people who can hold a broad range of emotions inside. So we can be spontaneous and uninhibited around them because we learn that very few things we do push them to an emotional place they cannot tolerate. And we also observe that in living their own lives such people can move freely in many different directions—in their work and relationships, for example—as their needs and desires change, without their having to pull back from what they want or need because of emotions they cannot tolerate. So we vicariously enjoy their freedom as an example of what living a fully human life can be like.

There is no more worthwhile agenda we can have than to work at enlarging our emotional capacity throughout our lives. One aim of every essay in this book is to enhance your capacity to do this. As life happens, we react with some degree of pleasure or pain, perhaps with a blend of the two. The pleasure may be joy or excitement. The pain may be anger, shame, or sadness. With some possible rare exceptions, all of us share the same repertoire of emotions. What sets us apart from each other is the extent to which we can hold them inside, identify them correctly, and then act or not act in ways that best serve our interests.

As infants, we have relatively little capacity to contain our own emotions. As pleasure or pain builds up inside of us, we start to move in all directions like wind-up toys, until we exhaust ourselves. This aspect of our emotional life never changes. Emotions remain calls to action throughout life. But we are not alone. Our parents provide what British psychoanalysts named a *holding environment*. They help us contain our emotions, but we don't know this is happening. We subjectively experience the process as "My feelings build up, the tension mounts, but before it gets to be too much for me, something happens and the tension starts to go down." What happens is that Mommy puts a breast in my mouth or Daddy picks me up and holds me, but what I experience as an infant is the buildup of tension and then its containment before it gets out of hand.

Like an athlete getting into shape, the more repetitions you have of this experience, the more it becomes a part of your nervous system, the more automatic it becomes, and the more your strength increases. In this case it is the strength to hold emotions, to keep them from bursting out into random action. For some of us this infancy-conditioning is inadequate, and even as adults we still launch ourselves into actions that others can see have a driven and random quality. We are talking, but the words seem to be just vehicles for our communicating our distress in a frantic effort to pull someone in to help us contain it. We are considering plans, but we zip through them at a pace too quick for us or anyone else to evaluate them. We seem as though we need to do something, but neither we nor anyone else can tell what that is, what would help.

When we are confronted with people in this emotional state, we experience a pull to do something parental—hold them, yell at them, send them to their room until they get it together. But we cannot do that with other people, so we often end up trying to talk them out of feeling so angry or hurt. We treat the distress as the result of bad logic and try to convince the other person that, according to our good logic, there is really no reason for them to be so upset. If, instead, we intuitively sense that what we are talking about is real distress, we may be able to create a holding environment with our words. These, however, must be holding words, not arguing words. We might, for example, simply say, "This conversation isn't working very well, is it?" Or, "I'm not getting what's important to you here, am I?"

There are people, however, who will be too difficult or complicated for most of us to manage no matter how sincere an effort we make. These are interesting words to apply to someone: *difficult* and *complicated*. They sound like descriptions of math problems, but we use them to describe people who are easily pushed by everyday interactions into emotional states they can't manage. We can't see them try and fail to contain and do something useful with a distressing feeling they experience. What we see is often what happens next; that is, we see them directing disappointment or anger at us for not being able to do it for them.

Fame

Andy Warhol has been quoted many times for his comment that in contemporary society we will all be famous for fifteen minutes. Actually, we are all famous for five years, the years during which we inhabit that little world of our family with few intrusions from the larger society. Then we get thrown out there and have about eighty years to try to get back what we have lost.

What, if anything, can we do that will lift us out of this crowd? We never give up this hope. We just get more subtle about it as we get older. But in children it is naked. I have never met a child who did not long for fame. There are no such children. But there are also no such adults, just adults who have had the desire beaten down in them enough in the competition of growing up so that it has become small and almost invisible.

But it is never gone, this belief we all harbor that there is something about me that is not like all the rest—and today at the office or on the softball field or in a clever comment made over dinner, it showed through. For a moment I could see it, and someone else saw too, and it was wonderful.

The art of small-time personal fame lies, so far as I can tell, in judiciously managing how much time and energy is put into its pursuit and also in remembering how little investment anyone else can be expected to have in your fame.

Practice Dying

Plato recommended that we not wait passively for the end, that we practice dying. It sounds like a most unnatural idea, but actually the natural rhythms of life provide us with regular opportunities to do that.

The process starts early in life. A child sooner or later bumps up against the limits of the self. This self, as we have come to call it, cannot even hold all the feelings that emerge from inside the child's body, much less protect the child from all outside forces. Mother adds an extra added dimension of protection, but even taken together, the mother and the self are vulnerable. Death will just be the last disruption.

When the emotions get to be too much—when their childhood rhythms take them too high or when events push them beyond tolerance—the self (maybe the soul) defends itself through what has been called "a blind damping down of the whole inner world." British psychoanalysts—most passionately

D. W. Winnicott—have argued that such damping down is especially likely to occur when anger or the wish to destroy someone who is frustrating us threatens to get out of control. In that sense this damping down is a sign of healthy development, a self-regulating ability, a thermostat with a safety turnoff switch.

We experience this growing ability in our children with a sense of both relief and sorrow. It is a relief because they don't fly into a rage at the slightest frustration. At the same time, however, it introduces into their life periods of withdrawal during which they seem out of our reach. Instead of coming to us for comfort or attacking us for not making them feel better, they move into a psychological healing space within themselves.

We never outgrow our needs for such periods of withdrawal and shutting down emotionally. Suddenly, we may find ourselves becoming serious, doubting ourselves, even feeling hopeless. We want time to think, but the thinking is slow and labored. Children may, at such times, complain of vague physical symptoms in their attempts to put into words what is happening inside them.

We worry about these moments in ourselves and each other, but they are what Plato ordered—opportunities to practice dying. If we view such withdrawals as self-healing, we can understand that it might be best to leave each other alone during such times for as long as the self-healing needs to run its course. Often, however, what happens is that when someone we need withdraws into herself, we want her to come back as quickly as possible. So, we often intrude on each other's periods of self-healing and contemplative withdrawal.

Letting the people you care about most get away from you when they need to is one of the more clever things you can do in a relationship. When they feel like that, they are least inclined to appreciate how much you need them.

When Life Doesn't Work

A big part of being human is our ability to imagine how things might be. Some psychologists have speculated that infants quickly develop the ability to hallucinate the breast. Once they have this ability, they do not need to have the real breast in their mouth immediately upon feeling hungry. They can wait a while. But, alas, a hallucinated breast will only go so far. It merely extends the time Mom has to get there with the milk.

This hallucinated breast, however, is a precursor of a lifetime process. We spend a great deal of our mental energy imagining how things might be. And once we create an illusion that we like, we experience a wish for life actually to be that way. Since life started out with a person who did in fact make the hallucination (of the breast) real, we continue to associate other people with the fulfillment of our illusions.

They could do something to help us make our illusion of a better life real. If things are not getting better, *they* are frustrating us. We are always referring to this anonymous "they," the world of other people who, as far as we and our illusions are concerned, are either part of the problem or part of the solution. If we are feeling good, we are likely to assume that *they* are okay, and if we are feeling bad, we are likely to assume that *they* are disappointing us in some way. We know when we are being satisfied and when we are being frustrated. We can feel it in our guts, and when we are being frustrated, we know someone else is involved in this.

It takes constant effort and attempts at self-discipline and self-regulation to experience disappointment, frustration, and disillusionment without seeing *them* as the culprits. To acknowledge that some adult version of the breast will never come, and to go on in the face of that without hatred toward some imagined bad mother who is withholding it from us, is a remarkable human achievement and a rare one.

We look better at handling this disappointment than we are because we have invented certain social devices to hide the hatred. The most common device is to spend time, after a confrontation with someone who has made us feel bad or failed to help us get some good feeling we want, explaining how something he did pushed "a button" of ours and now we realize that we have to deal with "our issues" and we "really" had no reason to become quite as angry or upset as we did.

He, in turn, may own some of the responsibility for the argument or disagreement with statements about being under pressure or not having seen how sensitive we were to some subtle and disguised aspect of his behavior. But this is storytelling.

We are jointly making up a story that allows us to go on together. We might more simply say that we can hardly stand it when we experience anyone getting in the way of our illusions of how life should be or when any interaction with anyone makes us feel worse in our gut and chest and throat instead of better. We can hardly stand it and have to work all the time to maintain a facade of acceptance and to keep from lashing out in anger, with the fancy language of adulthood disguising the complaints of the child inside us. And on this particular occasion now being rehashed, we simply did not stand it and stop ourselves from pouting or complaining or attacking. And it will happen again, because nobody bats a thousand in this league. We don't say that, because it leaves us nowhere to go, whereas the stories we create together after a falling-out allow us more latitude as characters and also allow us to leave the stage gracefully, able to return again for a later act.

Whoever Is Happy Is Right

We used to take the place where we lived for granted. There was a sense that America had become homogenized. Cities were cities, towns were towns, neighborhoods were neighborhoods. Then regionalism made a comeback. Now we don't just look for a place to live. We seek a sense of place.

It's never entirely clear why these psychological shifts happen. "Certainly it's true that since there is so much in the world now, it's harder to judge what is and isn't essential, all the way down to where you should live." That's how Richard Ford's fictional character the sportswriter put it, and maybe it's no more complicated than that.

Whatever the reason, we are in a period of time that is much different from the one in which the following piece of wisdom was offered: "Where you are is of no moment, but only what you are doing there." Or this one: "A true man never frets about his place in the world, but just slides into it by the gravitation of his nature, and swings there as easily as a star."

The essence of the shift may have something to do with the first of these two thoughts. We have come to feel that not everything worth doing, or at least not everything that makes us feel happy, can be done in every place. Each place has come to be viewed as an array of opportunities and constraints. On that basis places can be ranked and rated as to what they allow us to do and how they make us feel. One book I recently came across rates about fifty different cities in large part on the basis of how many days each month the weather will allow you to be outdoors in shorts and a short-sleeved shirt. Other schemes emphasize a specific range of factors.

Psychology Today ranked the nation's metropolitan areas on the basis of their rates of alcoholism, suicide, divorce, and crime.

The editors of *Money* magazine, by contrast, claim their readers tell them that what makes them happy with a place is a low crime rate, the likelihood that house prices will appreciate, and the availability of physicians. Like many place-raters, they also factor in the number of sunny days, but unique to their rating scheme, they came up with a measure of civic pride. Their definition of this intangible quality of life in a community is the percentage of its adults who have registered to vote. Their argument, completely unsupported by anything resembling evidence (as is often the case with place-rating schemes; it's really more like arguing politics and religion than it is like research), is that people show, or at least reflect, their commitment to their city or town or neighborhood by registering to vote.

Savvy Woman magazine even rated the best cities for women. The best was Seattle, on the basis of such factors as cost of living and housing and the percentage of women executives and managers. Pittsburgh scored third, with a crime rate that the magazine's local expert claimed was "lower than Cedar Rapids, Iowa," plus "a thirty-six-acre park on three rivers, enormous civic pride, small-town values, and big-city amenities."

Pittsburgh was also a surprise big hit with the 1985 edition of Rand McNally's controversial *Places Rated Almanac*, placing number one in the nation, ahead of San Francisco and Boston. Pennsylvania filled out its dark-horse winner status by placing Philadelphia fourth in this influential rating effort. Alas, however, such fame is fleeting. In the 1990 *Places Rated Almanac*, Seattle was rated number one.

Not everybody agrees with this preoccupation with where to live. "Stop searching," Ford's fictional character went on to say. "Face the earth where you can. Literally speaking, it's all you have to go on." A friend of mine made a similar point when I was going through a period of wondering if I was in the right place. "This is adolescent stuff," he said. "You have to live the life you have. This place stuff is just the wish that what there is will not turn out to be all there is—that there must be another and better life waiting around the corner."

This, however, is definitely the minority opinion these days. So I have been listening to patients and friends talk about it, and I can't see that any of the place-rating schemes really have much to do with how likely anyone is to feel happy with the place where they end up living. We react to places more the way we react to potential romances and marriages. Some things about the other person pull us powerfully toward them and some repel us, while most of what could be measured about them doesn't make much of a difference one way or the other. That's why so many of us recognize that we have ended up being happy with someone who isn't much like the person with whom we would have said we would be happy before we met this real person and became attached to them. And as Tolstoy so cleverly observed, "Whoever is happy is right."

Similarly with places. To make the relationship between a person and a place work, there must be some things that are powerfully attractive about it or the rest won't matter. And if there are a few things that are compelling enough, then the limits of the place won't ruin it for us. No relationship offers every opportunity. Some things will never happen in certain human relationships, no matter how much one or the other person wants them to happen. You either live with that peacefully, get bitter, or leave. And not all geographical, cultural, and recreational experiences are possible in every place.

We vary enormously in what we demand from another person to make us feel we are at home in a relationship. We vary just as much in what and how much we ask from a place before we will commit to it. Some of us are not willing to put down roots anywhere. Some of us have very specific items on a must-have list before we can settle into a place. A number of people I've met in Denver simply cannot tolerate a place that has no riverfront, no lakeside, no beach anywhere in sight. They have a bottom line and that's it. Others of us don't have a strict bottom line. We want one or two out of a broad range of pleasures, and if we happen to end up, maybe for job-related reasons, in a place that offers a couple of them, we'll feel right at home and never be inclined to leave. Then too, some people just don't leave. They marry once and that's it, no matter what. Others need a bit of trial and error to find what they want. On the second or third try they land in the right spot and stay put.

The one thing that we all must do to find peace with a place, or a man or a woman, is be willing to surrender opportunities and pleasures we once rated highly and accept some constraints and limitations we once thought intolerable.

Once you get past that hurdle, you might be able to milk the place for all it can provide.

This takes time, and is, therefore, a gamble. You might discover that no matter how hard you try, you and the place you're in cannot make it. And while you are finding that out, you may sacrifice some other part of the dream of your life. There are losers in this process. It doesn't always work out—because of bad luck, bad guessing, or inflexibility. *Esquire* called the unlucky and disconnected ones, who never feel they have arrived at home, "the wanderers." They never achieve a sense of place. "They are always dreaming of and searching for the one place that will provide the opportunity of belonging and give the days of their lives a feeling of context." They are life's permanent visitors to the homes of those who have found places, "homes where the spirit can really flourish, where a visitor is truly warmed, and where the owner can find solace for his own soul."

Maybe regionalism and the place-rating fad will fade again, and few of us will have much to say about where we live. But the underlying reality of how places affect the quality of our lives and how we know when we are home, and when we are not, is part of the human condition. It is a very old issue, and there is no way to be objective about it.

When Moses and the Israelites came to the borders of the Promised Land, after forty years of wandering in the desert and the wilderness, ten of the twelve scouts Moses sent out came back and said they had just seen the South Bronx of ancient times. They said it was a land that "devours its inhabitants." But Joshua and Caleb seemed to have come back from a completely different place, despite having been on the same scouting mission. They said they had found the proverbial land of milk and honey, with rivers, green hills, and fruit trees. Rand McNally probably would have fired those two guys and rated Israel the worst place to live in the world, but the Israelites called it home. Two thousand years later we still can't agree on the best place to live, but, on the whole, we don't search with any less determination. Place is still a potentially magic ingredient in the creation of an individual and family life.

Civil War

Skirmishes at the Fence

As we build our life, we erect an imaginary fence around it. As our experiences accumulate, we place each of them either inside or outside the fence. Inside are all the actions we are allowed (by our internal fence-keeper) to perform. Outside are all the actions we will no longer do. In fact, in most instances as soon as an action is placed outside the fence, the very possibility of doing it is pushed out of awareness.

The reason for placing an action outside the fence is always the same: the fear of emotional pain. "If I let myself become aware of my anger at my mother, she would see it too, and then I would really be all alone." "If I love a man, he will dominate and betray me." "If I attempt to finish what I start, I might produce shit." So instead, "I let my anger leak out in all my other relationships, including my relationship with my-self"; "I find a fatal flaw in every man I meet and end the relationship before I get hurt"; "I act lazy and confused and

47

nothing ever gets finished, but I can tell myself it might have come out okay if I had finished it."

So as life goes on, we begin to live as if there are thoughts we cannot think, emotions we cannot feel, and options we can no longer exercise. Keeping these possibilities outside the fence makes us feel secure. But the security eventually proves to be an illusion. Life confronts us with these possibilities over and over, and whenever they come close to the fence, we are threatened. So instead of dealing with the big anxiety in a showdown, we fight constant skirmishes all our lives.

Every theory of psychotherapy has zeroed in on some aspect of this universal phenomenon. Family therapy, for example, works on the idea that in every family we agree not to say certain things for fear that the family would fall apart—like a corporation in which everyone knows something is happening that shouldn't be happening but no one wants to say anything because then they will all be out of a job. To an outside observer who has no stake in keeping awareness of the secret outside the fence, the family members look insanely blind to what's happening. Even an overtly psychotic parent's most bizarre behavior can be reframed by other family members into something understandable for fear that to call this spade a spade would literally destroy the family.

Years ago, Rollo May discovered that among women who had been rejected by their mothers, those who admitted this suffered less anxiety than those who denied it. Once the deniers pinned their security to keeping the thought "My mother has rejected me" outside the fence, anything that threatened to make them aware of this reality became a danger. So danger was everywhere. A common strategy among those of us who are trying to avoid the knowledge that we were rejected by one or both parents is to please others so well that no one will leave us. Being left now would be unpleasant and painful as an experience in its own right, but even more painful would be the memory it might evoke of having been rejected by a parent when we were dependent children.

As Rollo May understood so elegantly in his book *Love and Will*, what we are seeking when we erect our psychological fences is freedom *from* disturbing emotions. This is nowhere more evident than in the unspoken, highly cautious strategies developed by many divorced and single people in their thirties and forties. When examined in psychoanalysis, most of these strategies turn out to be a variation of one theme—"How can I minimize the risk of disappointments, broken attachments, and betrayals?" But, May argues, the meaning of life lies precisely in the apparently insane mix of emotions such as love, loneliness, and rejection that characterize all relationships. When we are in a period of our lives during which we are outside any intimate relationships, everyone who has such a relationship seems to have found some magic way to keep the balance in it tilted in favor of good love and satisfaction rather than hurt and disappointment, whereas we are convinced that were we to let ourselves become attached, we would have the opposite experience.

Love, May has long been telling us, is the human answer to death. We say yes to opportunities to love and we believe rather than doubt simply in order to face death. Several older persons have said something to the effect that they don't much regret anything they did, but they do regret a lot of what they did not do. Loving is the biggest "yes" in human experience according to May. If it's not real, it's still a great myth. It is "the mythos of care. It is a statement which says that whatever happens in the external world, human love and grief, pity and compassion are what matter. These emotions transcend even death."

When we develop, as children or as hurt adults, the habit of lifting as little emotional weight as possible, it does temporarily spare us the pain that is part of developing any muscle. But it also pushes bigger and bigger chunks of life out of bounds, and we get more and more out of shape emotionally. The key piece of wisdom in May's psychology is that the whole point of the game of life is to bring inside the fence as many emotions and actions as you can before you die. The most free person is not the one who is free *from* anything, but the one who is free *for* everything.

To Do It or Not to Do It

There are usually more good, solid pieces of psychological wisdom in a single issue of *Outside* magazine than in a year's worth of most of the psychology journals to which I subscribe. One of the best was a story by Randy Wayne White in 1979. During a brief shore call on an Outward Bound sailing course, he made the decision to leave rather than complete the trip. As he hoists his duffel bag up onto the docks, one of the course instructors demands to know just where he thinks he's going.

White says, "First, I'm going to eat some fish at El Cacique, then call a friend at the sheriff's department and get a ride to my car—it's that simple."

The instructor demands to know why.

"How's this?" White replies. "I'm twenty-seven years old, and I want to leave."

And he did.

There have been many times when I have asked a patient

describing being trapped in an uncomfortable situation, "Why don't you just leave?"

As often as not, the question is puzzling at first. "It's not that simple."

But, as White wrote, it is that simple.

It just doesn't seem that way.

"No, I don't think I'd enjoy doing that." "I'm not interested in doing this anymore." "I'd rather not."

A few years ago, after having spent seven years building up a substantial practice doing neuropsychological testing with patients known to have or suspected of having some form of brain dysfunction, I abruptly stopped offering that service and limited my practice to psychotherapy. Most psychologists dislike psychological testing. It's repetitive, gets routine after a number of years, involves a lot of mechanical administration and scoring of tests, and always ends with the burden of writing a report at home (hardly any psychologist I know manages to get these reports all done at the office). The reports inevitably begin to feel like homework assignments, and, like homework assignments, they get left until the last minute when the referring psychiatrist or neurologist calls and says they are needed tomorrow.

Several physicians who had referred patients to me for this service over the years simply could not process the statement "I'm not doing testing anymore."

"What do you mean?"

"I'm not doing testing anymore. I've stopped as of January first. I'm just doing therapy now."

"Well, would you do this case?"

"No, I'm not doing testing anymore."

"I could see about getting you paid up-front."

"Well, ending up not getting paid on many cases was one of the reasons I gave this up [you don't have a relationship with someone else's patient whom you spend a day testing so the patient may put your bill at the very bottom of his bill-paying pile; or if his insurance company ends up paying the bill by sending the money to him, he may end up keeping it, and there isn't much you can do about it, unless you are into lawyers and collection agencies which I'm not]. But it wasn't the only reason. I'm just not doing testing anymore."

Sometimes it ended there, and sometimes they needed to try a few more times before switching their referrals to another psychologist. For a few it bordered on the inconceivable to jump ship when the rest of the gang was staying on for the duration.

Doing what you want. Saying no. The reason Randy White's story makes good reading is because his behavior is out of the ordinary. It is simply not what most of us would have done under similar circumstances. A number of completely insane marathon psychological weekend seminars have been able to count on a full house for the whole course because of the simple fact that most of us will not get up and walk out of a torture chamber with an open door if someone in apparent authority says, "Where do you think you're going?"

This is true despite the fact that one of the most straight-forward pieces of psychological knowledge about human nature is that whenever you continue doing something you want to get away from instead of changing course and doing what you want, you will feel sick for as long as you keep doing what you don't want.

That doesn't mean giving up a race because it hurts to run. Or that it's psychologically unsound to make a sacrifice for someone you love by temporarily doing something you don't like. It's quite possible to feel pain or discomfort and still want to be doing what you're doing. We can all tell the difference between that pain and the sick feeling of wanting to stop but staying on for what seems like "forever" because of group pressure, self-consciousness, fear of being humiliated by someone in authority, fear of getting a bad grade, fear of not getting the money we will get if we stay.

All those reasons are understandable, but do not change the fact that it makes us sick to keep doing what we don't want. Often it makes us physically sick. In fact, as time goes on, I become more and more convinced that when someone has chronic and unidentifiable physical complaints, the single best question to ask is "What are you doing now in your life that you do not want to be doing?" The next-best question is "What is there that you most often dream of doing but never genuinely take a shot at?"

This is the best definition of soul sickness I know. And most of us simply wish it weren't part of the human condition to feel this sickness when we do what we don't want or stop short of taking a shot at something we dream of doing. If it weren't, then we could pursue money without it costing us anything, we could do what makes "sense" without having to factor in that gnawing feeling in our abdomen and chest, and we could keep a lot of other people happy without making ourselves sick. It just doesn't happen to work that way.

This might come up more often in psychotherapy if problems with work and money were as integral a part of most psychological theories as difficulties with love and relationships are. As I have become more aware of this lately, I routinely see instances in which what makes the most sense to say to a patient is: "Look, I'd like to help, but that chronic feeling of dis-ease and distress you report is what we human beings experience when we spend our lives doing something we don't want to do. I realize you have children for whom you are responsible, and car and mortgage payments to make, and that you may not be able to find your way out of this trap without you and all the people you care about making sacrifices you don't want to make and don't want to ask them to make, but as far as I can tell, you will continue to feel bad as long as you keep doing something you don't want to do, five days a week, forty-eight weeks a year."

This might be bad for business. But it's the way human beings work. It's that simple.

PART TWO

CHILDREN, PARENTS, AND GROWING UP

Be Happy, Nobody's Watching

One of the genuinely liberating and happy outcomes of a good analysis is the gradual discovery that nobody cares about us to the extent that we once believed they did. We grow up imagining that people have an enormous investment in what we do and don't do. This illusion is a result of the reality that our parents experience us as reflections of them, so they often take what we do personally. But that's it. It ends there—for the rest of the world, but not for us.

On the other side of the emotional fence that runs around every family lies the world at large. Its inhabitants look at us and mostly shrug. At times they may need our cooperation to get something done. A few may become attached to us. If they need our cooperation and we don't give it, they feel frustrated. If they become attached to us, they will hope for some caring concern from us. Unlike our parents, however, none of them will be watching us all the time.

Being watched by parents is a major fact of a child's life. "Oh, look at what she just did. Isn't that cute?" "Do you know what I saw your son do today?"

Our parents watch us like hawks. So we keep thinking that people are watching us and really give a damn about how we do everything we do.

Our parents also register emotionally how well what we are doing matches their expectations for us and their need for a certain type of son or daughter. And we, in turn, register their reactions. The whole process of being cared about, watched, and treated as an extension of someone else inflates our awareness of ourselves as actors on the stage. This inflated self-consciousness is a huge burden, but we all start out our adult life bearing it. In that sense all young adults are a bit paranoid.

Some of us never dump that burden, and continue to feel the pressure of those ever-watchful parental eyes. Life remains a performance for which we never quite feel well rehearsed. We're sure we are supposed to be playing our part better than we are doing, and we are constantly aware that everyone watching the play knows we aren't getting this right.

Others somehow, either through self-realization or through therapy, come to see that they are much more alone in the world than they had imagined and that no one is watching anymore. When this breakthrough happens, there can be a sense of loss that the audience is gone and you are alone on the stage, but it also is likely to make you feel giddy with delight. This once-frightened child peeks out from the place where she's been hiding and sees that the watchers are gone. She's alone. She can be silly or spontaneous but, from now on, will be much less vigilant.

How the Inner Child Works

Most psychotherapies revolve around the concept of the inner child, even if they avoid that specific language as being too trendy or too unscholarly. It is simply a recognition that what we learned as little people about what makes us feel good and what makes us feel bad (and what is safe and effective to do about each) largely determines our *modus operandi* as big people among other big people. Because of this, whenever two of us are together, there are always at least four people in the room (when two very complicated people get together, there may be a cast of thousands operating). And without a score-card to help you identify the players, it can become impossible to understand what is going on.

When I gave a talk to some college students recently, the one scenario that led to the most grinning and head-shaking was that of a young man and woman deciding where to go for dinner. The situation gets complicated because the child inside each person is trying to get what he or she wants without appearing to be trying to do that and while simultaneously trying to make sure that the other person doesn't end up unhappy. Meanwhile they are both starving to death.

If childhood were simple, what would happen would be that each of us would learn what makes us feel good and what doesn't and we would discover effective ways to communicate those two states of ours to other people. What happens instead is that we become tricky. Most of what we are doing and saying with each other as adults is trying to get our needs met, but the inner child is cautioning us to be very careful to disguise these attempts so that it doesn't look like that's what we are doing. At the same time we want others to know what we need and to respond to our needs and desires, and we get frustrated when they cannot decipher the secret code of our communications.

I think that's why children love toys like the secret decoder rings they used to mail you if you drank Ovaltine and watched the *Captain Midnight* show. It's what they are doing in real life—learning to code their communications. That's how you can tell when someone's inner child is running his show instead of his adult self—you feel as if you need a decoder ring to figure out what messages his words and actions and body postures are sending to you.

I came across two examples of this recently that brought the concept to life for me and, I hope, will for you. One involved a real child and the other two inner children.

The scene with the real child took place in a park. I was trailing behind a family walking back to their car. Out of the blue the daughter, maybe age nine, announced that she forgot to turn in some type of school project on which she and her parents had been working for some time. Now, she believed, it was too late, and she would get no credit for it. My guess is that she just wanted someone to say, "Yeah, it would be lousy if you put in all that work and got no credit for it. Can you think of anything useful to do at this point? Can we help in any way?" Maybe then she would have been able to suggest, on her own, that she might turn it in anyway and see what happens.

Instead, the parents panicked. They began to talk as if it were their neck on the line here, as if they were the ones who were really in trouble. They mounted one good argument after another for why she had nothing to lose, and possibly, something to gain, by handing in the project even though it was late. She became more and more insistent that late is late and for late projects you get no credit, so the die was cast, the water was under the bridge.

That's how fast the roles of child-in-need and caretaker can shift in a relationship. As bad as she may have felt about not getting a good grade, they appeared to have felt worse. Further, the only hope they had of feeling better was her agreeing to turn in the project even though it was late. Their inner children were now trying to get an actual child, who was already in need of their help, to help them.

Out of frustration with this turn of events, she became angry at them and started to communicate the message of "Well, that's what we get and there's nothing we can do about it, and now our 'A' will turn into an 'F' in that class and we'll just have to live with it."

Age makes no difference in this inner-children business. That child is ageless and can even relate to actual children as if they were adults.

The other story involved the inner children of two adults. These "four" people were on vacation, and one got hungry and told the other, who was driving. The driver's inner child had in mind taking the passenger to a "perfect place" (inner children love to stage perfect events for those they love and get very disappointed if the other person's actual needs get in the way of their plans) for lunch, but it was twenty miles away. The hungry adult didn't want to wait another half hour to eat and would have settled for a greasy hot dog if it was available right now. But the driver's inner child had this plan.

So the hungry person suggested maybe a small snack, perhaps some ice cream, to cope with the hunger pains while they drove the twenty miles to the perfect restaurant. The driver's child agreed, but then remembered a perfect ice-cream parlor about fifteen miles down the road. Well, this inner child was so into the fantasy of the perfect place to eat that nobody was going to get fed until they got there. When they pulled into a gas station along the way, the hungry person finally had to drag out her child and have a sort of temper tantrum, because the driver's child—like the actual child with the late project—was not going to hear any type of logical adult argument.

If logic is going to work, it works right away. If it doesn't work right away, the chances are that a child has sneaked into the middle of some adult interaction and until that child is addressed—as a child—nothing is going to happen. What most therapists have learned to do is simply to step back and say, "Hey, you're really excited or upset about something. What do you need from me? What, if anything, can I do to be of help?"

It's a great tool. We should be taught to memorize it in high school, if not sooner, so it's automatic. We just say it when we get stuck with someone we care about. Sometimes the other person answers in a clear or disguised way (such as a series of "yes, but" responses to any suggestion we make) that she doesn't believe there is anything helpful we or anyone else can do or that, for some reason, she wants to remain trapped in her distress. Then all we can do is acknowledge this and maybe say, "Sounds like you're stuck with something pretty miserable. That's too bad."

We never get away from these children inside us. We might

all be talking to each other like Mr. Spock if we did. But like real children, these inner children do not always know what is making them happy or angry, or, if they do, they don't always know what to do about it. But the whole story of what is happening in most of our daily interactions reduces down to those three elements: who is feeling good, who is feeling bad, and what they are doing about it.

Who You Are ·

We all carry around in our minds a picture of ourselves. To survive emotionally, this picture must be one we can tolerate. Something about it must provide at least minimal self-esteem. When someone enters psychotherapy of any type and the therapist asks him what has brought him into treatment, the answer is always a description of this inner picture. The patient or client really has no choice but to start talking about that picture if she is to say anything at all to a stranger about her life. What will not be so clear is what she likes and doesn't like about this picture.

A man may say, for example, that he dislikes his temper, while also feeling that his ability to intimidate others is something he likes about himself. With great predictability, the very complaints that bring people into therapy will also be descriptions of aspects of their inner picture of themselves that they value.

One increasingly common example of this is the high school student who abuses drugs. If the parents bring the adolescent to a therapist, here is what will almost invariably happen. The adolescent will admit the drug use but will claim that it is not a problem. "I do it because I want to, not because I need to. I'm in control, but my parents believe I am out of control." To reformulate that inner picture of himself from that of a person in charge of his life to one who has become dependent on a line of powder or dried-out plant leaf would mean giving up so much self-esteem that the picture of himself in his mind would now be so demeaned as to be hardly worth keeping alive. So that adolescent is fighting for his inner emotional life when he says he does drugs because he likes it.

In addition, this adolescent is likely to have become enmeshed in a social group composed of others who use drugs almost constantly when the group is assembled. They literally would not know what to do with themselves if they did not get stoned or high first, and that adolescent has no place else to go. Parental injunctions notwithstanding, to make new friends is a lot easier said than done. So if that inner picture is viewed without drugs, it immediately becomes a picture of someone alone, without a peer group. No adolescent would trade a peer group for no peer group.

What can the therapist give the adolescent to replace what all the adults want the adolescent to give up? Nothing. So psychotherapy with such adolescents has been singularly ineffective. By contrast, self-help groups like Alcoholics Anonymous and Narcotics Anonymous have emerged as reasonably effective treatments because they allow for the creation of a new inner picture—one that is enlarged to encompass the fact that the drugs or the alcohol are too powerful for this person, but without this apparent "weakness" being experienced as something to be ashamed of. Everyone in the group is admitting the same "weakness," and soon the new member of the group sees that admitting the weakness is a strength. In addition, this admission cements her belonging to the group, whereas in the world outside the group she feared such an admission would mean alienation and humiliation. Now the picture of the addicted person or the alcoholic is a picture of someone as human as anyone else, courageous, and part of a secure and loving group.

That's the self-image we all want to have. And we will continue to get it where we can. If larger proportions of adolescents are finding it in drug-abusing peer groups rather than in schools or families, then a smaller percentage of classrooms and parents are providing it. The messages on television are directed to the easiest target to address. It's easy—not useless, just easy—to remind kids that drugs destroy lives. It's harder to think of thirty-second messages that usefully inform parents or educators about ways they haven't already thought of to create homes and classrooms in which more children can develop inner pictures of themselves that make them feel good. It's harder, but it is one of the most important things that grown-ups can do for children. Because as a society of parents we have not seriously taken up this task as a high priority, we are left as individuals to manage it as best we can. With that problem in mind, what I refer to as the wisdom contained in these essays can be viewed as tools with which to cultivate the kind of adult attitude that helps us raise children who have self-images that sustain them without the props offered by other children in drug-abusing peer groups.

Dysfunctional Families

It did not surprise me to read in a popular book on dysfunctional families that the author believes most families are dysfunctional. The dysfunctional family is the newest theory that attempts to explain why so many of us have such profound difficulties in living happily and with a sense of well-being.

Like most similar theories that came before it, dysfunctional parenting originated as a way to explain the behavior of a specific group of people seeking professional help, in this case adult children of alcoholics, many of whom suffered from the disease themselves. And as has happened with all similar theories of psychological disorder, its adherents gradually came to believe that this theory explains almost everyone's adult unhappiness.

The common starting point for all these theories, from Freud's to Bradshaw's, is the observation that an awful lot of us suffer from chronic bad feelings such as anxiety and shame, and as a result we develop defenses that make our lives more miserable than they ought to be. Invariably, it comes to be speculated that bad parenting left us with the bad feelings, and that to avoid the bad feelings, we developed the maladaptive ways of relating to others and thinking about ourselves that now have us stuck in a psychological rut.

None of these theories has really been proven in any definitive way to be better than the others. It's mostly a matter of which theory's language you find best captures your experience. What does seem to be beyond a doubt is that things are getting worse. Despite all the persuasive theories and the proliferation of child therapists and clinics and the books for parents, the well-being of American children is declining.

The most important recent national report on the state of our adolescents revealed worse school performance and more delinquency, drug and alcohol use, teenage pregnancy, and self-destructive behavior (especially suicide) even in the supposedly privileged group of sixteen- and seventeen-year-old white adolescents under study than was true of similar children twenty years ago. It was supposed to have been the opposite because things got significantly better in large social terms— less poverty, smaller family size, and better-educated parents— the three factors that sociologists believed would make things better for children. So it ends up appearing that even when the society at large gets more comfortable and affluent, we still are "screwing up our children."

The question that never gets asked, or at least never gets answered, is why as an entire species we should have turned out to be so inept at this fundamental task of raising children. What exactly is wrong with us? There are two ways to look at this. One is that the smarter we get, the more stupid we get. Some architects think that's happened with the way we design the places in which we live and work. In the beginning the people who used the space designed it. Then we invented professional architects who partly want to create nice spaces for us but also are artists who want to express their visions and do something innovative when they design our home or office. So we end up with novel buildings inside of which we feel lousy. The architect-critics have simple advice: "Hey, remember that the idea is to create towns and homes and buildings that make us feel good." They walk around the building site with the people who will use it and ask, "How would it work if the main entrance was here?" or "How does it feel if we do it like this?" So maybe we do the same thing as parents. Maybe, when we were at our best in the "the old days," we just used to let children hang around with us and we treated them nice. Now we believe we are at our best as parents when we manage our children's upbringing with a lot of professional input, and in the process we don't make them feel so nice.

The other possibility for why we can't get parenting right is that we don't really care that much. Part of what it means to be human is being fundamentally self-centered. A lot of good theory-making these days points in that direction. Mostly, we all want to pass on our genes and reach the maximum in our own personal self-fulfillment. From time to time we push at each other to think more about the other guy, and occasionally we all do, but mostly we are just simply human and narcissistic as hell. So it's not really that surprising that while, as a group, we adults have been making things better for ourselves in the last twenty years, our commitment to our children appears to have weakened—with the result that their well-being isn't doing too well, even among the white middle-class adolescents in the study I mentioned earlier.

Now it occurs to me that maybe I've contradicted myself here. First I seemed to be saying that we have turned parenting into a field of scholarship. We have become obsessed with doing it right. In that sense, we might be viewed as caring too much. Then I argued that maybe we don't care very much. Well, I want to let that contradiction stand. It's the most real thing about us as parents, that we care too much and too little. We want everything to turn out right for our children, but we want everything to turn out right for us too. We want them to feel good and we want to feel good, and sometimes those twains meet and sometimes they don't.

This is obviously going to be an uphill climb for as long as we are raising children on this earth. Making things better for children is only one of many competing personal and social priorities, no matter what we sometimes may say about our children being the most important part of our lives. In one national survey done in the early eighties, two out of three of the adults questioned said that "parents should be free to live their own lives even if it means spending less time with their children." We pay our money and we take our choice.

The single best thing I ever heard about what children need was that every child needs to feel that at least one adult is crazy about him or her. If you're crazy about someone, you want to spend a lot of time with that person, and if two thirds of us really think that "living our own lives" is different from spending time with the children we create, then children will increasingly bond to each other instead of us, and raise each other, as many do now in the private enclaves of adolescent drug-oriented social groups. It would be something if we someday discovered that all children want is to be allowed to hang around with us and be welcomed even though they act like kids.

How Much Guidance Do Children Need?

One of the few psychological experiments that strikes me as having discovered something genuinely useful was called *the cafeteria experiment*. Young children were allowed to select all their own food by going through a cafeteria line. At first, as all parents fear, they ate only what they liked. Soon, however, they tired of this unbalanced diet and selected more foods from previously neglected food groups. Eventually, they constructed a balanced diet all by themselves.

The idea that children will regulate themselves if left alone can be generalized to most areas of their life. As psychoanalyst John Bowlby has put it in his classic series of books on attachment and loss, "From the earliest months forward it is best to follow a child's lead. When he wants more food it will probably benefit him; when he refuses, he will probably come to no harm. Provided his metabolism is not deranged, a child is so made that, if left to decide, he can regulate his own food-intake in regard to both quantity and quality . . . [and] in regard to mothering—as to food—a child seems to be so made that, if from the first permitted to decide, he can satisfactorily regulate his own 'intake.' "[1] For the first three years of life, he is not spoiled by receiving as much parental attention and presence as he seems to want. After that, he will naturally develop other interests, and his demands for parental time and attention will gradually lessen.

It seems to work well enough to let children do what they want unless there is good reason to interfere. Too often the reason for interfering is our own discomfort and not the child's needs and well-being. I want to bring this closer to home. I've been watching our oldest daughter struggle her way into a college major. She was a great high school French horn player who found out that in college all the other girls with music scholarships were also, by definition, great high school horn players. Now, however, the question was which of them, if any, would become great college and professional horn players and play first chair for a major city orchestra as they all dreamed of doing. Well, after a while she began to communicate a realization that she had "eaten" enough horn for one lifetime, thank you, and would now be trying out something else. Well, there went the scholarship and that whole career. Then our family moved, and she wanted to try a different college in the part of the country to which we had relocated, and we all knew that this wasn't how I had done it, nor how her mother and I had ever expected she would do it. She didn't want us to be disappointed. We didn't want to be disappointed—whoever has said to their child, Please disappoint me in some really major way so I can say I had that experience during this lifetime? She fantasized about one ca-

[1] John Bowlby, *Attachment*, New York: Basic Books, 1969, pp. 356–57.

reer after another for a year, like one of those cafeteria kids going down the line checking out all the offerings, and sometimes she turned to me and asked me what I thought she should do or if one of the careers she had noticed that week looked good to me. Keeping this idea in mind—that she had somewhere inside her the capacity to know what tasted good to her and what she needed—got us through the suspense and helped to keep me from rescuing her by trying to find inside myself the certainty and decisiveness she couldn't find for the moment in herself. She ended up taking an interest of hers— photography—that had remained steady throughout her life and reclassifying it from hobby to career. Then she found a college at which to study it, and she was on her way again— her own way.

The bottom line is that there are situations where the answer can only come from that place inside us where we know what tastes good or what we need, and no one else has access to that place even though we might like them to at moments when we don't. So if we lose touch with it, we just have to wait it out until the connection is reestablished, and then we have that feeling that our Self, with a capital S, is back on the line, and we can say, "Gee, I'm glad you're back. I've been needing to ask you what we want to be when we grow up. Ah, yes, a photographer. Of course. Well, I'll go do that now."

The Body and Adolescence

Freud reminded us that we have bodies. It might seem odd that we would need to be reminded of that, but periodically down through the centuries we have forgotten. Through some blend of Enlightenment rationality and John Locke's argument that human nature is a sort of blank slate waiting for experience and external stimulation to mold it, people in the late 1800s had begun to talk as if the body were just a thing that carried out the bidding of the mind. We could be whatever kind of creatures we wanted to be—no limits.

Every generation, of course, adolescence proves Locke wrong and Freud right. Sex throws our two genders up against each other, and our allegedly rational minds seem to collapse into our bodies. The world is suddenly filled with irresistible human sights and shapes that were never there in quite that way before. We can't stop talking about the ones we find most attractive, but, to be safe, we can only have these conversations with people of our own sex, thus further isolating us from the bodies in which we are really interested. With rare exceptions—such as Texas high school football players and girls whose fathers see in them the next Jennifer Capriati— little else really matters except wondering which of those desirable bodies your body is attractive enough to attract. So getting through physics and world history and into Harvard is really even a more amazing feat of self-discipline than it seems.

It would be convenient if adolescence were just a passing phase, but it really isn't, not, at least, the part of it I'm talking about here. Our bodies remain in the foreground throughout life, but we learn a few more tricks to thinly disguise our preoccupation with them during some of our interactions.

Despite this, there is a particular outcome that is especially life-limiting. It's the one in which sexual adolescence remains a permanent state, and we end up with adult boys and girls who see people of the opposite sex mainly as overpowering seducers or who are preoccupied with those aspects of their bodies most sexually important to the people of the opposite sex.

It's part of the work of adulthood to understand that we all have bodies, sexuality, and gender to cope with and enjoy. If we are competent at dealing with these dimensions of being human, we even have a shot at that special brand of intimacy that only men and women can share.

A large part of the terror of adolescence is precisely the fear that we will discover that we are incompetent at dealing with this part of the human agenda, and as a result will not only be embarrassed but also alone. And by this I mean alone not only in the sense of being without anyone of the opposite sex for company, but alone in the sometimes worse sense of having to settle for someone we don't want to be with because we can't get any of the ones we do want. And one way to deal with the anxiety and humiliation of that perceived incompetence is to develop what I would call a *gender role*. You can be incredibly competent at school and work. Then, in your fantasy, you will be loved anyway even though you aren't grown up and competent in the area of sexuality and intimacy. Or you can be overpoweringly sexy and maybe no one will notice that you're terrified of sexual relationships. You can even be overtly incompetent and dependent so that someone who needs that kind of relationship will want to be with you in order to take care of you. The roles are endless, but they all keep you outside the realm of real adulthood because you are not working to get more competent at handling body-sexuality-gender-intimacy. Instead, you are playing a safe but unsatisfying scene over and over and knowing that adolescence was the end of the road for you. Equally tragic, you know that, by definition, you only pursue or open yourself up to relationships with men or women you don't really want to be with, because in order for them to be with that adolescent version of you, they must be stuck inside the adolescent version of themselves also.

Many good courses of therapy end with the patients feeling that while they have got unstuck, that is not the same as being catapulted into adulthood. They are ready to move out of their adolescence, but they haven't done it yet and don't automatically have the social skills that would make that easy. The dilemma in this situation is that it leaves two tough choices. Find another recently unstuck and ready-to-grow-up person with whom to move forward (that would make a wonderfully honest personal ad) or find someone who is ahead of you in the growing-up process and see if you can use what he knows without becoming his permanent junior partner.

Mommy and Daddy

I was twenty-seven the first time somebody called me "Daddy." She wasn't my child, but I had no children and she had no one being her father, so I guess she saw the wisdom of not wasting time. Eventually, I became her father, so she may have been prophetic as well as wise.

The word froze me inside and I'm sure I didn't respond, but from that moment on I could never again fit comfortably inside the boyish identity that had carried me through until then. I felt immediately pushed through a time zone and into a space where all the men my age with no such relationship to a child faded into the distance. It was like my notice from the draft board in 1967 to report for my physical. There was time-before-the-letter and time-after-the-letter. Those were the only two kinds of time.

Women have told me that they experienced the same feeling when the child of a man they were dating began to think of them as Mommy. If it was for them the first time a child perceived them as Mommy, they have had that same reaction: "Who, me?"

Now, as I write this, my wife is about to deliver our third child and first boy. Each time the jolt is the same. During her pregnancy I lapse into a state of denial.

As I've watched other couples have their first child, it continues to amaze me how impossible it is actually to know what parenthood is going to feel like until it happens. The excitement we feel when we learn that our first child is on the way doesn't mean we know what is actually about to happen. What that excitement is like is this. During a wonderfully undefined year after college, a friend called and told me that the Ph.D. program in which he was a student had scholarship money to give away, and if I applied I was sure to get accepted and get thousands of dollars a year just for studying. That, he was sure, was better than driving a cab (he was dead wrong). I applied and got accepted into this program, which led to a Ph.D. in biopsychology. At this point I still had absolutely no idea what biopsychology was about, but that didn't stop me from feeling excited.

Ever since then I've sort of mistrusted that excited feeling. It doesn't necessarily mean I know what I'm doing, especially when my wife tells me she's pregnant. The people running the biopsychology program sent me a letter telling me about my admission into the program and giving me the option of accepting or rejecting their offer. My wife has not, so far, sent me such a letter at the birth of any of our children, and I suspect that my requesting one from her might create bad feelings.

I think the trouble occurs when we assume that being a real grown-up who is ready to parent a child means having a complete, predesigned agenda for parenting. It doesn't mean that at all. A grown-up attitude toward parenting is reflected most clearly in a readiness to learn what the particular child we are about to confront will turn out to need from the two of us. This not being able to know ahead of time is scary. So books that tell us what to expect from the average expectable child are comforting while we are waiting. But each real child invents us as Mommy and Daddy all over again.

As a result, none of us, not even those of us who are great at being grown up, know ahead of time who we will become as the mommy or daddy of each child. That's the enormous power of children—to redefine us to ourselves and, by telling us in this redefining process what they need in a mommy or daddy, to push at us in the most profound way to find in ourselves or develop anew aspects of ourselves that they happen to need.

I remember a family I met while working at a child-development center that specialized in helping families with severely disabled children. The mother and father had had an unusual dream of including their first child in the world-travel type of life their careers happily allowed them to live. Then this child actually came along and couldn't walk. And they were told he never would. And they were at that moment, by their own definition, totally self-centered and committed to not having their hard-won and perfectly customized life disrupted by a child but rather having the child accommodate them. But this child needed parents with a completely different set of priorities, and so he invented them, and this man and woman became them and spent four years in the face of constant medical advice to the contrary teaching that boy to walk unaided—and finally he did.

The dramatic examples are, of course, easy to respond to. But the point holds in ordinary families. Children will—must—try to reinvent us to meet their needs, and will make every effort to do this. I think that this is what grown-ups who have children are emotionally prepared to tolerate and what nonadults who have children find most difficult. I am not saying that good parents allow themselves to be completely reinvented by a child. What I'm saying is that they tolerate the child's effort to do that without communicating, overtly or covertly, that they resent the effort itself. It's what children do.

Puer Aeternus

Puer aeternus—eternal youth—is a phrase taken from Ovid's *Metamorphoses* and used, especially by Jungian analysts, to refer to a person who cannot give up adolescence. This problem has been traditionally thought to afflict mostly men—thus the masculine is used generically—but my own experience suggests that it's just as prevalent with young women.

Such adult adolescents live what one author calls a "provisional life," always feeling that whatever is at hand is not yet what they really want. No man or woman, no work, no place to live, is quite right. It cannot be right, because all significant life choices mean you get something and you give up something. No place is better than every other place in every way. No career allows you to do all the interesting things that can be done during a lifetime. No relationship with a woman or man provides all the satisfactions possible.

Any romantic relationship can, if you indulge in such evaluations, be seen to fall short along some dimension. It may fail to provide something already experienced with some other man or woman. It will certainly fail to fully deliver something you imagine to be attainable in greater quantity or better quality from some other relationship.

Adolescence is the time before such choices, when all things are possible because nothing has yet been decided. All adolescents will not settle for mediocre mates but will marry the most wonderful man or woman, live in the most desirable home and town, and do the most interesting work. The *puer aeternus* clings to this stage of life and is unable to commit to anything actually available. All romantic partners, for example, turn out to be ordinary human beings, not the sought-after goddess or hero and never the longed-for emotional savior.

"The one situation dreaded throughout life by such a type of man is to be bound down to anything whatsoever. There is a terrific fear of being caught in a situation from which it may be impossible to slip out again. Every just-so situation is hell." That's how Marie-Louise von Franz captured it her her superb psychological study of the adult male struggle with the paradise of childhood. But although she happened to be reporting on her experiences with men, the adolescent inside anyone stuck in this personal myth can easily be detected by the telltale endless stream of protests ready for all occasions: "You never told me I'd have to stick to this job even during boring periods" is just one example.

It's easy to make fun of this, but it's just as easy to see the universal human struggle with our capacity to dream. We don't *choose* to dream about an extraordinary life. It's part of being human. But I believe the key to letting go of the particular version of the adolescent dream each of us writes for ourselves is seeing the role that the desire to be envied plays in keeping it alive. After all, what is it about the versions of ourselves and our lives in these fantasies that makes them so desirable? What makes them feel so good? By what criteria would we be able to tell that we had risen above everyday insignificance into this special state? Only when others say in some way, shape, or form, "Gee, I really envy your marriage, children, house, car, career, fame, status, creativity, or your whole package." Or at least when we imagine they do. Most people resist this idea at first—that they are looking to be envied by others—but it's often there. It's just a trait that, despite being widespread, is also widely viewed as something to be ashamed of. So we learn to cover it up and deny it. But it's there, and it's the hallmark of the adolescent version of the great life: I have a life that others would love to have but don't have.

The adult version of the *puer aeternus* dream may have some of the same components in it, but it's less driven and urgent because the desire for envy has been factored out or diminished. For the adolescent the possibilities are either to be one of the envied or one of the pitiable enviers. For the adult there's a third choice: the pleasure of crafting a life that fits well around the shape of your core self and then living in it with the certainty that what makes it so right for you is that no one else would want one exactly like it if given the choice. It's precisely that no one else really wants it just that way that makes your dream, and whatever approximation of it you can realize, the natural cornerstone of your adulthood.

Going Home Again

Although I had heard the title of Thomas Wolfe's book quoted a hundred times, it was never entirely clear to me why everybody seemed to agree so readily that it's a universal truth that you can't go home again. I figured it might help if I actually read the book instead of just quoting the title along with those other people who probably had read it and, therefore, knew why quoting it made all heads within earshot nod automatically without a shred of skepticism.

It turns out that Wolfe's book has an unwritten subtitle. You can't go home again if you tell the truth about what happened there when you were growing up.

A big part of being a member in good standing of any group is that you agree to whatever lies the group needs in order to maintain its collective self-esteem. In Wolfe's novel George Webber has written a novel about his family and hometown. When he returns home with his usual "Hi, guys, what's new?"

attitude, he is shaken to discover that what's new is that he's an outcast.

Fifty years later psychology has discovered that all families lie. In fact, children and adults probably couldn't survive together in the cramped emotional space of the nuclear family unless they lied to each other.

Nature has helped children lie effectively by equipping them with the mental ability Freud called *repression*. If the lie is important enough, the truth that would unmask it can actually be forgotten. That way you don't have to monitor yourself constantly to make sure you don't let the truth slip out.

Of course, children also lie when they know they're lying, and they know they need to do this, no matter what we tell them about how it will be better for them if they tell adults the truth all the time. In *Prince of Tides* Pat Conroy's narrator, Tom Wingo, reminds his children of this universal truth in an unforgettable scene. "Remember what I told you . . . parents were put on earth for the sole purpose of making their children miserable. It's one of God's most important laws. Now listen to me. Your job is to make me and Mama believe that you're doing and thinking everything we want you to. But you're really not. You're thinking your own thoughts and going out on secret missions. Because Mama and I are screwing you up."

Parents, of course, lie back to their children. It would be embarrassing not to, because we're all at least a little crazy and guilty and embarrassed about what we are sometimes doing to our children, while getting away with it because they are little and we are big. So after we do one of these crazy things to them, we tell them that something else just happened, not what they might think happened if they were watching and using ordinary everyday logic to assess what happened.

In the early years of psychoanalysis this wasn't so obvious because the focus was on discovering all the ways we do distort what's going on. Eventually, some analysts began to recognize that, while that may be true, it's also true, maybe even more true, that the process works the other way around. What we call children's fantasies are often children's fairly accurate, but metaphorical, accounts of crazy family events made more confusing by the lies that are used to explain them.

So when the time comes to move from being a child in the family to being an adult among other adults, the leap can only be made if at least some of the previously unspoken truths can now be talked about. The adults have the most to lose in this process because, despite the impossibility of it, we expect to be much better at relating to children than we turn out to be. The truth would expose us as the screwers-up of our children. They, of course, would be the innocent victims. That's what they think at least when they return home to have it out.

I've been talking so far about grown-up children as "they" and "them." I've been thinking about myself and you as parents. Now let me switch hats and talk about us as the children going home. Most of us know that we can't go home and really "have it out" because our parents still won't admit the truth, the whole truth, and nothing but the truth. And, in the end, we really don't want them to—for two very good reasons. First, it would be devastating for any of us to have our childhood idealizations of our parents completely undone. We all have identified with our parents. We secretly believe ourselves to be like them in many ways. We know that often the very things about them we dislike the most have become parts of us. We can hear their voices when we lose our tempers with our children. We hear their way of talking every now and then when we are at ease with friends. We even have this peculiar sense of conviction that the brand-name products they used at home are somehow unquestionably the best, the standard against which all other products in that category must be judged. We have met our parents at their worst and they are us. As I once heard a colleague put it in a conference about a patient, "We get even with our parents by becoming like them." And so, if they are reduced to nothing, we know we will not be far behind.

But there is a second reason why we don't want our parents to tell the whole truth. Part of that truth would include an honest account of everything they have never liked about us. Who is better positioned than our parents to have witnessed our unique brand of being manipulative, dishonest, selfish, lazy, arrogant, miserly (and wasteful), petulant, and otherwise fully and miserably human?

So when we do go home, as grown-up children, to visit our parents, we head for the refrigerator or plop down in front of the TV or find any number of ways not to do what we do when we are with our friends, which is talk about our lives and how we experience ourselves and how miserable we feel and how we attribute some of this misery to our having been screwed up by our parents.

The only way in which we can go home again is if we and our parents can tolerate some of the truth. I've seen some people—not a lot, but some—go home again, and that's how they did it. The children talked their way back in, and fortunately the parents showed some genuine curiosity about what it was like to have been their child.

Those are the two necessary ingredients: adult children who are willing to turn off the TV at their parents' house and say something about their lives and who they have become and parents who can tolerate the truth. A rare combination, unfortunately, but something to shoot for. After all, we didn't pick each other the way we pick our friends, and there's no reason to assume it ought to have been a perfect match.

There's a great scene, in a play or novel I can no longer

identify, where a bitter son more or less tells his father that his father shouldn't have participated in bringing him into the world if this unhappy life was the result. The old man looks at him quizzically and says, "I didn't know it was going to be you."

Satisfying Mother

No one can study psychology without reading a great deal about mothers. But the comment that sticks most firmly in my mind came from a family therapist whose name I can no longer remember. In a magazine interview she said that you need to be in a relationship with your mother in which you are neither her agent nor her enemy. I think she was talking to women about them and their mothers, but the wisdom applies to all of us.

I have become convinced that every child and adult with whom I have worked in therapy or analysis started out life with the top item on their agenda being satisfying the desires of their mothers. They all learned to understand these desires in more detail than they learned to know their own desires.

We all start out this way, as the agents of our mother's desire. What does she want, and how can I see that she is satisfied? This is life's number-one question for all children.

Fortunately, there are happy and secure mothers. You would never know this from reading Alice Miller or John Bradshaw, but these women do exist. And they have managed to communicate to their lucky offspring the idea that satisfying Mother is not the number-one priority in life. Mother can take care of herself emotionally. If she needs to be taken care of emotionally at times, she will seek that from people of her own and older generations.

Some mothers, however, don't give that message, and it is the face of that mother that has launched a thousand diatribes. As all the newer psychoanalytic theories emphasize, contrary to Freud's vision of development, every child's safety and security is rooted in the feeling of being loved by a woman who tells her children that their ways of loving her and being angry at her are acceptable. To keep contented whichever woman we get in life's first great lottery, however, all of us as children will willingly sacrifice our personal desires, feelings, thoughts, and actions. . . . Having gradually lost contact with these pieces of ourselves, we emerge into adolescence and adulthood unable to set a clear and satisfying direction for our own lives.

If we discover that what makes us happy makes mother unhappy, then good and bad have been fundamentally and perversely redefined for us. *Good* is supposed to be that inner sense that tells us, "This is me, this is right for me, this satisfies me." But now we have a powerful reason to relabel all of that as *bad*. "What makes me happy is bad" is the worst outcome of this conflict. A common version is simply that "what makes me happy might be good or bad for me or her," and I don't have any idea how to know the difference, so I can never decide or move.

Out of this dilemma came the notions of the good self, the bad self, and the false self. Instead of our immediate experience leading to a feeling of this is good and right for me or this is bad and wrong for me, every experience has to be filtered first through some other person—real, or kept in our minds precisely for this purpose.

We are then saying, "Never mind how this feels to me. How does it feel to you?" There is no way for anyone to win in this scenario. If I do what you want, I have kept in your favor, but I am angry and resentful at once again having been forced to sacrifice my own desires. If I do what I want, I am convinced that I have caused you to become less content. Then there is less of that happy you from which I draw my emotional supplies, and I am, therefore, deprived in the end anyway. I can never win. Nothing I do ever increases my sense of well-being.

Eventually, I may construct what many psychotherapists have come to call a false self. A seven-year-old girl to whom I administered an intelligence test for one of my graduate-school courses saw mine and called me on it. I never really liked this part of being a psychologist, the administering of standardized tests according to strict instructions that have to be followed rigidly every time. She tried to lighten me up and relieve her own anxiety at being with a stranger by telling me funny stories. I would respond with a contrived smile and a sound that I imagined resembled laughter. Finally, she said, "What you do. That isn't laughing. You do this." And she mimicked me perfectly. "This is laughing." And she told another funny story and really laughed at the end. That got me laughing, and then I was really there with her, telling her some jokes I knew and having a good time.

We all have a false self, and we can use it to orchestrate larger movements of our lives as well as an isolated moment with another person like the one I just described. Overtly successful careers and marriages in which everything appears to be running smoothly can suddenly collapse when the false self runs out of energy and can't keep up the pretense anymore. The more our ambitions, our attempts at loving in our own way, and our attempts at hating in the way we hated as children have been met with humiliation, attack, or emotional abandonment, the more of our life this false self is likely to be running. In place of the passion and the force of our own unique destiny that our real self would rely upon for making decisions and taking major actions, our false self uses a game plan for running the show—a script, as some psychologists have called it—so that there is the appearance of consistency and direction that other people expect.

But this false self is just a character I have created. From time to time the real self wakes up and is depressed to find that "someone else is living my life. What happened to me? Where am I? How come I am not acting out there in the world? Why am I up here in the loft operating this puppet down in the world of other people?"

The answer is always the same: because I believe that puppet has a better chance than I do of engaging other people and maintaining their love and interest. If during one of its awakenings the real self can drag itself and the puppet into therapy, or can, through a monumental act of will, hang in and refuse to go back into hiding, the healing process may begin.

Some of us never come out of hiding, and entire lives are lost, without ever having been known to the rest of us. When I have *lost* patients like this, have been unable to keep them from returning to hiding, have watched them leave with mutual regret, not with anger, but with a resigned sense of "Thanks, Doc, but this is too much for me; it's too late for me," I experience the deepest sadness I know in my work. It's like watching someone bury himself or herself in a quiet ceremony for two.

The Me I Don't Want to Be

In 1947, one of the first child psychologists, Gardiner Murphy, had this conversation with a three-year-old girl named Joan:

> "Who are you?"
> "Joan."
> "Who is Joan?"
> "Me."
> "Is this Joan [pointing and touching bed alongside]?"
> "No."
> "Is this Joan [touching her slipper]?"
> "No."
> "Is this Joan [touching her leg]?"
> "No."
> "Is this Joan [touching her head]?"
> "No."

This last response clearly startled Murphy, who was sure Joan would think of her head, as the container of her thoughts, as being the seat of her *self*. But Joan described her head as *hers* but not *her*.

Then he rubbed his hand around her belly and lower chest and asked again: "Is this Joan?"

"Yes."

Five days later the same conversation took place, and again Joan "was found to be still in the same place, the belly and lower chest, but not in the head, neck, arms, nor back, nor dress, nor shoes."

The chest and belly are where we register our most powerful feelings: from joy and excitement to shame, guilt, anxiety, emptiness, and grief. And when the bad feelings grow to a point that we feel is more than we can bear, our reaction is to wish that we were not ourselves, that we were someone else, anyone else, anyone with a body that, at that moment, was free of those torturous bad feelings.

Most suicide attempts, I believe, are carried out within the unconscious fantasy that *I* can kill off my *self* while *I* will continue to exist. *I* don't want to end my own total existence, but *I* want to rid my *self* of that thing in my belly and chest that seems permanently filled with bad feelings, the pain of which *I* can no longer stand.

Freud's final theories take little account of this piece of the human experience. What Freud chose to emphasize was that feelings lower down the body—feelings of sexual arousal—are the main part of life with which the mind must grapple. Rather than human beings having minds that control their bodies, they actually have bodies that determine the primary agendas of both their conscious and unconscious mental activity. That was Freud's revolution, and a hundred years ago it was an even more radical conceptualization of the human psyche than it is today.

But Freud could not be expected to see everything there is

to be seen about us. Later psychoanalysts were forced by the needs of their patients to include more of the body in their thinking about what it is inside of us that drives the mind and sometimes drives it crazy. They had to include Joan's belly and chest.

Now we realize that the most critical part of helping a child grow up is to help that child become capable of managing those feelings that haunt the body and chest, especially in bad times. Otherwise we will have a person who frequently wishes not to be in his or her own body: that is, wishes not to be who he or she is.

The psychological capacity to manage such feelings is developed by children in relationships with adults who—because they don't get the child's bad feelings confused with their own—can continue to offer attention and affection during the child's bad times. This leads the child to develop the sense that we can manage bad feelings, often with the support of others who love us and, at times, by loving ourselves. Love dilutes the bad feelings and helps them heal.

There is no more critical business in families than helping children develop the capacity to form relationships in which the bad feelings will be met by love and support, and simultaneously to develop the ability to love themselves even when their bodies feel full of the most awful emotions.

It would perhaps be helpful if we could all, as new parents, have that conversation with Joan or some other child who reminds us that children live in their bellies and chests, not in their heads. They just want to feel good there.

PART THREE

MEN, WOMEN, AND RELATIONSHIPS

Valence

During a morning run through my neighborhood, I was surprised to see an older man I knew walking toward a corner mailbox about a half-mile from my house. He had, briefly, been a teacher of mine, and then, sometime later, I happened to end up playing poker with him one Friday night.

I hadn't seen him in a while, but the feelings in my gut reminded me that he mattered to me. Much as I had always pictured him in my mind's eye, he exuded a self-contained and tough attitude even while mailing a letter. I saw him, but if he saw me, he didn't recognize me.

I felt like stopping to say hello, but I immediately was aware that there was more going on than that. If I stopped, it would have been with the hope that I would get some sign from him that he was glad to see me. But I didn't think I mattered much to him. The threat of experiencing that disappointment threw me sufficiently off balance that I didn't stop and take the chance.

One of the key dimensions of all relationships is valence. You may recall, from chemistry class, that valence refers to the power of one element to combine with or pull in another element. In all of our relationships one person ends up with a higher valence than the other. That person is more important to the other. His love is more needed by the other person than vice versa.

Valence can shift during the life of a relationship, but its status at any moment will determine, as much as any factor, how the two people in the relationship dance with each other. The higher-valence person will lead.

In my past encounters with that older man whom I ran past on the street, he had a higher valence in my mind than I had in his. The difference in our age and our relative positions in the group activities that had brought us together before made it likely that he would end up with the higher valence, but all relationships operate on the same seesaw principle. The seesaw is never exactly level. One person is always at least a little up and the other a little down, at any moment.

This becomes obvious when a man or woman leaves a spouse or lover. The person being left immediately experiences an enormously increased need for the other person to value him or her, while the leaver experiences no such increase. It doesn't matter what the relative valences were before the leaver announced he or she was leaving. The threat changes everything. Some people leave just to reverse a valence that has been uncomfortably tipped against them. It gives them instant relational power.

In some relationships the balance of valence stays pretty constant. In others it shifts as rapidly as an atomic clock, and the two people have a hard time figuring out who is up and who is down. Once you become aware of this principle, you can see it operating all the time.

You know who, among your friends and co-workers, lets you lead the dance and whom you usually follow. You're in a conversation and you are relatively free to take the lead and say what you feel like saying or you are self-conscious and watching to see what the other, higher-valence person might like best. The higher-valence person can be himself or herself, while the lower-valence person is performing.

Because relationships work this way, some common behaviors are doomed to failure. In the painfully familiar scenario of one lover leaving the other, the "leavee" will experience the impulse to prolong the conversation during which the "leaver" has announced that the relationship is over. This, however, is absolutely the worst time for the leavee to have anything to do with the leaver. The difference in valence between them is at its widest spread, and the leavee's value at its lowest ebb.

Your best bet, if you are the leavee, is to leave or let the leaver go, and give the leaver a chance to experience the reality of the loss—to find out if he really will be happier without you, as he now believes he will be. Pleading your case at that moment is a no-win maneuver.

The same idea covers a multitude of other situations, and the principle is always the same. The worst situation for any of us is to need something from a higher-valence person who is hostile to us. The only more self-destructive act is to express the need. You risk blowing your feeling of dignity along with whatever little valence you have left. By definition, there will always be a better time later.

Doing Marriage

While I was teaching at a medical school, I noticed that some of the students collapsed under the weight of their own ambition because what they wanted was to "be a doctor," not to do medicine. Being a physician looks and sounds great. There's status, money, and the feeling of being an insider in a group that others wonder about with awe. But there is also the reality of first *doing* medical school and then *doing* the actual taking care of people who expect a lot and get angry when they don't get perfect care.

Some of the most depressed students were those who wanted medical school to be over with so the good times could start rolling, and who detested almost every assignment and learning task involved in the four years of study and training. Now, working with individuals and couples, another version of the same phenomenon catches my attention again and again. Many people want to *be* married without *doing* marriage.

This is a different reason for a dysfunctional marriage from incompatibility. There are many reasons why two people may be incompatible and may not notice that they are until after they have been married for a day or two. The only way to keep that reality from creating a significant number of divorces would be to go back in time and make divorce religiously or socially unthinkable. Or, perhaps, the increased attention being paid to how divorce hurts children and how unsuccessful many of us are in leaving one person to seek a more perfect union with someone else may discourage some from fleeing a discontented marriage. Neither social shame nor private guilt, however, will change the fact that some combinations of two people will inevitably turn out to form lousy teams.

The phenomenon I am getting at here has a different quality from this business of incompatibility that we have known about for a long time and probably cannot do much to avoid. What I am talking about here is the frequency with which we confuse wanting to *be* married and wanting to *do* marriage. The confusion is no different from the vocational confusion that plagued those medical students.

Being married is nice. Being married is just the part of marriage where you are a team instead of alone, where you have children who love you, where there's always someone to go on vacation with and have dinner with on Saturday night. Things like that.

Doing marriage is more complicated. It is a one-day-at-a-time proposition. It's not something you can *have.*

The decision to do marriage is the decision to gamble your life on an experiment. It's you saying, "I wonder what it would be like if I spent my whole life in a monogamous relationship with one man or woman." You can't find out until you get to the end of the experiment, which in this case is your life. Some experiments look like losers in the middle and then surprise you at the end. That's what make them experiments. If you quit in the middle, that's just another gamble—a gamble that you can tell from your experience of stages one and two how stages three through the end will go.

That means that when we ask each other about marriage, it should come out more like, "Do you want to try to start a marriage?"

Sometimes it seems to a couple that dating and living together are a good test run for doing a marriage, but when I have watched couples go from those activities to doing marriage, it never seems as if there is much of a carryover—not even as much as there is between spring training and the regular season for a baseball team (which is usually very little).

It is more like the relationship between high school baseball and pro ball. As with any human activity, a few of us turn out to be very good at doing marriage, most of us turn out to be good enough, and some turn out to be below average at it.

But that analogy doesn't fully capture this notion of marriage as a lifetime experiment, because life goes in stages that don't always have a lot of continuity. Maybe someone is not great at doing the first part of a marriage—such as being thirty-something and starting a family—but will be great at doing the rest of it, even dealing with adolescent children leaving home. You can't know ahead of time. You just find out as you go along. The decision to get married, if it is a decision to do a marriage as opposed to the very different decision to see what being married feels like, is the decision to run the experiment to the end and see how it turns out.

As we go along, some of us find out that we really had never intended to run that experiment, that we were thinking of a series of shorter experiments, which we have come to call *serial marriages*. You don't know how that sort of thing will end up either, not until the end.

If we continue to accept serial marriages as one of the options, then young people may be able to announce that intention or expectation when they enter a marriage—announce their intention to run one sort of experiment in living versus another, like baseball players negotiating contracts for a certain number of years. If it's a long-term contract, the team is gambling that you'll fit in and work out for a long time. If it's a one-year contract, they are saying they are not that sure of their long-term agenda and how well you will continue to fit in. And you as the player have the same choices to make. You might decide that you want to run out your whole career in one place, or keep your options open because you think that maybe next year you'll get a better offer.

We now have the option of free agency in marriage as well as in baseball. It makes it hard for the fans to feel safe with getting emotionally invested in a team, and I have become convinced that it makes it very difficult for children to feel safe with the stability of their families. Even in happy families that give little indication of falling apart, children are as intensely aware of the threat of their family exploding in their faces as they are of the threat of a nuclear war. It is now part of the backdrop against which their lives unfold, and that is the biggest difference between us and them, and, I suspect, the thing that has made their lot more difficult, much more so than the fact that some of their mothers work outside the home.

We are always deciding as a group how the game ought to be played, and just like the major-league owners, we can get together and change the rules. Each time we decide for serial marriage, we cast a vote for that to be an option for everyone in the league, and all the fans and players know it. Unfortunately, in this case, the fans are little and dependent and can't evolve fast enough to become creatures who are comfortable with that type of uncertainty. It's just another complication to be factored in when making the choice about how to run the experiment.

I think about this differently as my oldest daughter gradually moves into the time of life when marriage is a possibility. I can't imagine wishing her a happy series of marriages. But neither can I imagine some moral argument for the goodness of staying within something that is killing her emotionally. What I end up wishing is that she and whoever he turns out to be could get hold of the idea that marriage is an experiment and that to be honest they must at least start out saying to each other, "Look, I really can't predict who you will turn out to be as our lives unfold, but I'm willing to enter this experiment with you anyway. My commitment to staying in it isn't dependent on your turning out to be the embodiment of some half-secret fantasy I have of a husband or wife. It is dependent solely on my own sense of commitment and my sense of your continued commitment. As long as I believe that you are committed to doing this marriage with me today and maybe as far into the future as tomorrow, I'll stay and do it with you."

The Stranger in Your Bed

The stakes have got a lot higher in psychotherapy over the last thirty years. There was a time when the goal of therapy was change of behavior, elimination of irrational beliefs, or strengthening of the ego and reduction of inner conflict. Now there's a new ultimate goal. The patient should emerge with a true, coherent, and stable self. This "self" serves a function similar to that of its immediate conceptual predecessor in psychotherapy theory—identity. Both are terms for the sense we all have that there ought to be something consistent in the way a person experiences and manages life. Some people have more of this quality than others do, and when a person has enough of it, we view her as having a solid identity or a cohesive self. We have also developed various ways over the years to talk about what people do to compensate when they don't have enough of this quality. Often we say they play roles.

A role is prefabricated, ready-made, and mass-produced.

We see another person's way of arranging his life and we treat it as if it's ours. So a role is easy to come by but never quite fits. And, by definition, it's not very flexible. It's like a movie script in the hands of a very rigid director.

Anytime we enter a new situation in life, one in which we feel uncertain or anxious, we may, without realizing it, pull a role out of our unconscious and proceed to play it out. I had a teacher in graduate school who was very clear about the right and wrong way to handle each and every category of therapeutic interaction. This bothered me when we were in class, but when I was alone with a patient and couldn't think of anything useful to do, I found myself, often without thinking about it, using his guidelines and even his sample comments to patients. I could play the role of him doing therapy. It gave me something to do when I felt I (the real me) had nothing competent in mind.

Marriage is also a situation that we enter as anxious beginners. Even people who have lived together before marriage are still new to marriage when they make that change of status. It's a very common situation in which to adopt a role. We all have a model of husband and wife in our mind, built up over a lifetime of observing our parents and other examples of husbands and wives. We may not pay much attention to it before we are married, and some of us may feel comfortable enough even in the earliest days of a marriage to play things by ear and remain flexible and curious. But most of us cannot do that. The state of being married throws us into the role of husband or wife and leads us to have a rigid expectation that our partner will conform to the other role as we have it scripted in our mind.

Over the years I have worked with many couples who experienced a profound negative shift in the quality of their relationship as soon as they married. When they were dating, they could be more themselves. They seemed to have an identity and to be able to allow their partner to have one. They were still playing at how to be with a romantic partner, and their playfulness allowed them to generate as much fun as they are capable of contributing to a relationship. They were comfortable not knowing exactly how everything in the relationship should work.

As soon as they began to think of themselves as husband and wife, however, curiosity and experimentation didn't seem to be enough. They unconsciously believed they should know what to do and that there was something new and definite to do. They jointly became invested in being and looking like a competent couple.

Believing this—that there is a right way to be a husband or a wife—while also being afraid that they didn't know enough about that right way led them to adopt the role of husband or wife as they understood it from their families and from what they had absorbed of the most rigid cultural stereotypes. And, even more destructive, they began to expect their partner to fill out an image they had in their head of what a husband or wife should be.

All of a sudden these two playful characters are transformed into androids, preprogrammed to be, and to relate to, a predefined model of husband or wife. If an audience were watching this play onstage, they would think that during the break between acts the playwright had shown up backstage with a new script. The old characters have been replaced by two new and unrecognizable characters.

He is chronically disappointed and confused by her inability to get the role of wife correct as he knows it to be in his inner child's vision of life. Her little girl can't imagine how she mistook such a gray computer printout of a man for the full-color guy she thought she had. Now we have two kids who didn't get what they wanted for Christmas even though both had opened the boxes ahead of time and were sure they had seen exactly what they wanted.

One woman with whom I worked in therapy suddenly felt, after she married a man with whom she had lived for two years, that he was not decisive enough. In her mind the role of husband was characterized by a firm and decisive authority figure. The man to whom she was married had a different portrait of husband in his inner landscape. For him a husband worried constantly about making money and left all domestic and relational decisions to his wife. They both felt he carried his weight in domestic chores, but he genuinely felt no interest in the making of any nonwork decisions. Once these two people got curious about where the versions of themselves they had known before marriage had gone, they began to take steps toward letting go of the inflexible mental models they had of the roles of husband and wife. He could recognize that, in reality, his wife earned half of their family income and did not want to abdicate the role of worker and worrier-about-income to him. She began to recall that one of the things she had liked about him from the start was that he was a team player who could share control of decision making without feeling threatened.

There are other versions of these role switches. Someone becomes a physician or a psychoanalyst or an executive and really *becomes* those roles. As Joseph Campbell once remarked, such people can no longer laugh at those roles—one kiss of death in life—because they believe themselves to be those roles.

Maybe someday we'll all have clip-on video cameras through which we record our greatest dates or shoot films of ourselves before we entered professional schools or became spouses and parents. Then we could review them when we get stale—review them with a healthy sense of "Oh, yeah, now I remember, before I took this part, I was going to live my life."

Warming Each Other Up

"We rarely understand what the person next to us really wants, what kind of message he is addressing to us, what kind of confirmation we can give him of his self-worth. This is the problem of our most intimate lives—our friendships and our marriages: We are thrown against people who have very unique ways of deriving their self-esteem, and we never quite understand what they really want, what's bothering them."

The sociologist/anthropologist Ernest Becker made this observation in his book on *The Birth and Death of Meaning*, but we have all shared the experience. We rarely are completely aware of our own strategies for maintaining self-esteem, much less anyone else's. And, as Becker observed, on the rare occasion that we do break through and actually understand someone else, we are usually shocked by what, to us, is that person's peculiar way of looking at things: "Is that what's bothering you? I never would have guessed."

Despite this fact, we continue to expect better communication in our relationships, and we are usually disappointed when we don't get it. When I first studied Harry Stack Sullivan's psychology with his disciple Patrick Mullahy, Mullahy used to say frequently that Sullivan saw relationships as being like tennis games. We ought to be just warming each other up, hitting the ball back and forth in such a way that the other person can get to it. But sometimes we can't, because we don't know where the other person is standing on the court, and sometimes we don't, because we want to get some advantage.

So we have this experience with others in conversations where we feel like saying, "Whew, that one went right by me." Or, "Where exactly did you hit that one?" And, of course, "You rammed that one right down my throat, didn't you!"

It doesn't make us perfect players, but it helps keep the warm-up on track if we occasionally remind ourselves that the point is to keep the volley going, and to do that, the other person must be able to return what we hit.

Alone Together

It would be an interesting experiment for any couple to spend a day together without any deliberate attempt to communicate—two people who already know they need each other being together all day without talking or gesturing or doing anything that involves each other except looking at each other.

Moments when a baby is within eyesight of its mother but is not interacting with her have come to be considered the foundation for the capacity to be alone in adulthood. Baby is there but wants nothing, not even Mother's attention. Baby is alone, but in Mother's presence. Baby's aloneness is by choice.

As the children who have had such experiences grow up, they take this nonintrusive but present mother inside them, and that mother is a constant companion to them. Children who have not done this by school age often sit and wonder what their mother is doing while they are not with her. Children who have done it engage in such fantasying only rarely because they carry around a version of their mother with them that has enough of a charge—like a battery—to get them through the day. Each child knows how long he or she can go before needing to be recharged by engagement with Mother, but, for the most part, we don't care as much about these individual differences as we do about the convenience to adults of standardized and predictable school hours and schedules.

The nature of this kind of being alone doesn't change much as we move from childhood into adulthood. As Winnicott described it, "[W]hen alone in the sense that I am using the term, and only when alone, the infant is able to do the equivalent of what in an adult would be called relaxing." The relaxing person can flounder around inside himself or herself, directionless, not reacting to anything going on in the surrounding environment or initiating any activity with a goal. Such moments set the stage for the emergence from inside of us of what a Freudian analyst might call an "id experience," and what other analysts might think of as the experience of the true self. Whatever it is called, what such moments create is the possibility for some type of sensation or impulse "that will feel real and be truly a personal experience."

If Winnicott was right about this, and more and more psychologists are coming to believe he was, we allow each other far too few opportunities for such moments than might be possible. Since few of us will arrive at chronological adulthood fully able to be alone in this way, we still need some help from each other further developing the capacity. But often when one of us experiences being used by someone else in this way, it makes us uncomfortable. We have the sense that the person wants us with them—maybe in the same room—for some reason, but we don't know why. And she can't tell us. But I suspect that the reason is so that she can be alone—something that we only gradually learn to do by ourselves and that many of us need to do, at least every so often, in the presence of someone else.

Hate

If the British psychoanalyst D. W. Winnicott is right and hatred is universal, then it makes sense to have some very reliable long-term relationships within which we can hate safely without fear of total and irreversible abandonment. All good friendships and marriages are containers for hatred. The hatred can explode from time to time inside the container without destroying it, like the canisters used by bomb squads to allow safe detonation of an explosive.

Even the most loving parents also hate their children. Winnicott wondered if this hatred of which we are ashamed found disguised expression in the nursery rhyme:

> Rock-a-bye-baby on the tree top,
> When the wind blows the cradle will rock,
> When the bough bends the cradle will fall,
> Down comes the baby, cradle and all.

An odd set of lyrics for a song designed to comfort infants.

Many relationships come to a premature and unnecessary end when the first burst of hatred is interpreted as a sign that the relationship is bad, instead of being viewed as a sign that the relationship has become safe enough for one or both people to have released some of their hatred into it. "I trust you enough to hate you as well as love you." In that sense love means never having to say I'm sorry, because the hateful act for which an apology might seem in order can be understood as a love note. As long as the notes don't come every day.

Men and Women in Therapy

Gender abuses us. The concerns of life—power, sexuality, creativity, competition, knowledge, intimacy, independence, dependence, children, money, production, consumption— are spread before us like a menu. To be forced into or out of the activities connected with any of these concerns is the essence of all abuse. There is no inevitable reason for gender to function in this abusive way among grown-ups, but it always has. The desire to embrace large group differences and apply them across the board is a trait common to children: "I'm a Brownie, and you're not. I'm taking karate lessons, and you're not. I'm a boy and you're a girl, and that tells all there is to tell about us."

One aspect of adulthood is moving beyond such childish abuse, and the same quality ought to be a given in any therapy. But therapy has spawned its own versions of this abuse. Therapy, in fact, has been no less obsessed with gender than any domain of human activity has. Understanding how this happened in both therapy and psychology in general helps a great deal in seeing our way out of it, not only there but also in our individual lives. And finding our way out of it is, I believe, crucial to adulthood.

Men, it was long assumed by therapists of many different schools, were naturally aggressive, competitive, and achievement-oriented. Women were assumed not to be. So women who appeared to be were treated as possessed by unresolved masculine strivings.

All people, it was assumed, would naturally seek as much autonomy as they could have. But for many women patients attachments were a higher priority than independence. So they were viewed as pathologically overdependent.

The human conscience, which Freud called the superego, was assumed to be forged out of a boy's fear of being castrated. Girls didn't have to worry about that, so they were viewed as morally weak, willing to bend the universal rules of right and wrong in favor of their own situational ethics or even in favor of their own self-interest.

Less talked about was the corresponding treatment of men. If they were not aggressive and competitive, it was assumed they were neurotically inhibited. If their strivings for independence were not as much in evidence as desires for closeness, they might be viewed as passively feminine.

To correct these abuses, which arose from an overreliance on theory, therapists turned to research data for the truth—a sign, by the way, of therapists' desperation in the matter of gender, because therapists ordinarily don't put too much stock in the research findings of academic psychologists and sociologists. In these studies groups of male humans or animals were compared to female groups. The fact that in all such research there is a large degree of overlap between the two groups (despite differences between the groups as wholes) was rarely discussed. If, for example, sixty of one hundred women placed more importance on intimacy than independence, while sixty of one hundred men showed the opposite tendency, it would simply be said that men seek autonomy while women emphasize bonding. While the idea of distinct sets of male and female values or distinct male and female life agendas rescued some women from being viewed as sick or deficient because they valued interdependence more than independence, the question of what this implied about women who were not invested in caring relationships was left unanswered. If a woman shows little interest in marriage or children, is she deviating from a natural female tendency toward nurturance and bonding?

And this research didn't say anything about the place of aggression, achievement, and competition in the psychological lives of women. So therapists made up their own new theories about this. "Femininity" should be understood as embracing both aggressive and nurturant tendencies. Women plagued by guilt, depressive-like fatigue, and anxiety while attempting to "have it all" should be viewed as showing normal emotional reactions to the effort to live up to an impossible ideal, rather than being viewed as neurotically conflicted.

This new frame of reference was better than the old attitude, but ends up in a maze of contradictions. If, for example, femininity combines the aggressive and the nurturant trends in human psychology, what of masculinity? It is either the same—men want it all too—or it's now the lesser state with men only wanting to aggressively and autonomously achieve but not really having much natural interest in nurturance and intimacy. In that case we would simply be back at it again, dividing up the pie of human concerns, theorizing about how much of each slice men or women should be expected to embrace. In addition, as good as the "femininity equals aggression plus nurturance" formula appears at first glance, it is essentially a rephrasing of the current notion that women naturally want to have it all. What it adds to this notion is simply the interesting prediction that they will naturally burn out in the process of trying to have it all. So, where does that leave women?

This confusing and contradictory outcome is inescapable, in my view, whenever we try to reduce human questions to gender-specific concerns. The effort always self-destructs, as can be shown through a brief history of theorizing about gender and morality. I believe it makes sense to detour for a moment into this somewhat scholarly territory, because what gets said there inevitably ends up affecting the images of men and women that prevail in therapy and in the day-to-day relationships between men and women. Also, if our goal is to develop adult attitudes toward gender, then we need to know something about the origins and current attempts to bolster the adolescent attitudes we are trying to leave behind.

The key element in this story is that Freud's argument about women ending up at a lower level of conscience development than men was supposedly supported by academic psychological research that centered around the theories of Lawrence Kohlberg. Kohlberg compared groups of boys and girls at different ages in terms of how they reasoned when faced with deciding what the right thing to do is in situations he made up. He concluded that most girls stop at a level of moral decision making lower than the level most boys reach. At the highest level moral decisions are reached by applying universal laws of justice across the board in all situations, but girls' morality centers around nurturance and responsible care, and therefore leads them to decide that what is right varies from situation to situation. The classic example is that boys are more likely than girls to argue that it is justifiable for a man with no money and a dying child to steal medicine to save the child's life, while girls are more likely to argue for a resolution that works for all involved: arrange payments; avoid doing something that might end up with you in jail and your wife now having not only no money and a sick child but no husband to help her. The conclusion often drawn from this disparity is that girls fail to see the universal principle that saving a life takes priority over respecting rules about property ownership; that is, boys know that there are rules that apply across the board. This conclusion was not just part of an ivory-tower debate. Women learn it in college psychology courses and read it in newspapers and magazines, and to the extent that some bought it, they might easily question their own capacity to function, say, as a judge, if not question their general adequacy as adult coordinators of any important activity.

Just as women therapists began to challenge theories of masculine strivings and dependency needs in women, so did women researchers challenge Kohlberg. A new perspective crystallized around the work of Carol Gilligan, and especially her book *In a Different Voice: Psychological Theory and Women's Development*. Gilligan asked the kind of question that would occur to a therapist who was not caught in the obsession with gender: Why can't justice and care both inform moral decision making? That should have been enough said, but with gender there is always one more question: Why would it be the case that men and women, boys and girls, respond differently to questions about making moral decisions?

It is usually thought that Gilligan never took up this question. In a recent discussion of Gilligan's work, however, Joan Tronto points out that Gilligan does sometimes seem to be arguing that women's different moral voice might be "a function of their subordinate or tentative social position." That, of course, might make women's caring moral outlook a mere reflection of their secondary social status. And that in turn would mean that Gilligan might be arguing for the acceptability of a moral ethic of caring that, in fact, was only appropriate to people in a subordinate or minority status, and it might imply, as Tronto points out, "that Kohlberg's theory of proper moral development is correct, so that the failure of women and minority groups to develop properly is just a reflection of a regrettably unequal social order."

Of course, as Tronto continues, it might also mean that women are courageously clinging to their correct moral views even in the face of rejection of these views by the more socially powerful male group. Or it could be interpreted as reflecting the fact that people who spend a lot of time taking care of children, as women do, have thereby the chance to develop what is actually the higher form of morality—that is, Gilligan's ethic of care. From this last viewpoint Kohlberg just mixed up the order of the top two levels of moral development, and women are more moral than men.

That's another way that gender questions self-destruct, by lapsing into infinite explanatory possibilities among which there is no obvious choice. Rather than debate all of these competing possibilities *ad infinitum*, what Tronto proposes is that we simply take up the issue of how far one can go with a theory of morality based on an ethic of care rather than justice or care plus justice. What would be the possibilities and problems of a world in which this moral voice prevailed? It's another way of saying what I said in the first essay of this book. Life is an experiment. We can't know answers to questions like this in the abstract, Tronto is saying; we would have to try it and see. In this case trying it might mean trying it in our conversations about morality to see if an ethic of care and justice made sense, or we could try it in action by seeking to implement it socially.

And at that point in the scholarly debate, things have come full circle to the same wisdom that prevails in good therapy. Theories about gender differences in any area of human concern—moral decision making, aggression, autonomy, nurturance, achievement—really become subordinate in psychotherapy to an ethic of individual differences. The therapist accepts the more difficult road of finding out where any patient stands in relation to such human concerns as aggression or nurturance—how much any one person is comfortable with them, conflicted about them, or comfortably unconcerned with them. As a therapist, if I hear a woman reason morally according to an ethic of care rather than universal justice, do I then conclude, "Oh, of course, she's a woman. That's how women think"? Or if a man reasons morally according to that same ethic of care, do I conclude that he reasons like a woman? Neither conclusion is useful in my attempts to understand the subjective world of either such a man or such a woman. The only thing useful to me in all this is to know that there are these two ways of reasoning and that people vary in how compelling they find each way or how conflicted they are about allowing themselves to do it one way or the other.

In any research that uncovers large group trends, as all the research comparing males and females on any dimension does, the biggest danger is in forgetting that it is trend research, and is therefore not capable of generating findings applicable to all members of either group. Dukakis, it is sometimes claimed, lost the presidency for sure when he responded to that infamous question, about what he would want to happen to someone who raped his wife, in Kohlberg's male way—that is, according to a universal principle of fair justice for all (even for a man who has raped his wife), rather than giving a personal response specific to that situation, such as "I'd get a gun and shoot the guy" or "I'd want him to get the death penalty." Even the man who asked the question thought it was the wrong answer. What does that say about the whole gender/ morality debate when it's taken out of the sterile atmosphere of a research study and into the real world?

When we do forget that research comparing large groups of subjects never turns up absolute differences, but only relative ones that do not encompass the individual realities of all the subjects, then we begin to reason in oversimplified ways. Neither a series of psychotherapy case studies nor a research comparison of a group of men and women yields findings automatically generalizable to all men or all women.

Still, we make such generalizations and seem excited about the opportunity to do it. In a recent book review in *National Review*, for example, Nicholas Davidson concluded that "if men and women are different, then traditional society, in its broad lines, is natural. The claim that women are oppressed evaporates, and feminism stands revealed as an absurdity." The only thing revealed as absurd here is Mr. Davidson's reasoning, because what he means by men and women being different is that relative differences are found between large groups of them in certain studies. If research comparing males and females turns up differences of the type that seem to interest him—"concerning the role of the male hormone testosterone in aggression, the role of the female hormones oxytocin and prolactin in nurturant behavior, and the more recent discoveries of major differences in brain structure between men and women"—how does that lead us to conclude that traditional societies, in which all men and women were categorically pigeonholed into lifetime roles because of their gender, are natural? It doesn't. Even psychological differences that have roots in hormonal differences are not absolute. So, "traditional society in its broad lines," with men and women pigeonholed into roles on the basis of assumptions about what their biology best suits them for, cannot be defended by hormonal and brain studies. It's inconceivable that someone is still arguing that they can. Does this guy have any grown-up daughters, and have they called home recently?

Indulging the childhood desire to find our identity in large-group traits and applying large-group differences across the board violate the quintessential piece of wisdom of psychotherapy: Tolerate the uncertainty of not knowing who the patient is until the evidence of your shared experience gives you something useful to say. Taken to its inevitable conclusion, gender-obsessed, large-group thinking would lead to the creation of a therapist who might well think of saying, "Ah, Mr. Davidson, welcome to therapy. I see that you're a man. Kicked any ass lately, and if not, why so inhibited? Why are you resisting your testosterone?" Anyone who heard even a subtle expression of that kind of thinking from a therapist would immediately feel he was in the hands of an angry and nasty child rather than a competent adult. And he would be right, not only in therapy but anywhere in life. That's why our effort to make sense of this aspect of adulthood took us into a discussion of theories of therapy and moral development—the craziness about gender in those domains highlights and reflects the craziness about it that we all live with every day.

All therapy begins as therapy with an unknown person who gradually reveals herself or himself. Adult relationships and adult assessments of other individuals work that way too, or ought to. Such an attitude, by contrast with Davidson's appeal to the natural biological order of human life, reflects what sociologist Peter Berger and his colleagues correctly identified as our principal achievement as human beings over the past four hundred years: "the specifically modern discoveries of human dignity and human rights." The corresponding adult attitude that is embodied in all good therapy is the desire to make the most of every life, not to reduce lives in general to their least common denominator.

It's not easy to resist the temptation to enter the gender conversation, and in my first attempt to write many of the essays in this chapter, I tried it myself. It seemed exciting to take my shot at answering the question that spawns so many books and articles: What, beyond the obvious, is different about men and women? Like other attempts at this, however, mine left men who read it saying they often felt exactly the way I claimed only women felt, and women saying they not only often felt the way I claimed only men did, but wanted to shoot me for suggesting otherwise. This was especially true when I implied that some area of life was easier or less conflicted for one group versus the other. It simply became apparent to me as writer of this book, as it has been apparent to me as a psychotherapist, that if there is something to worry about on the human agenda, we will all end up worrying about it if given the chance: having children, raising children, making and spending money, sex, aggression, morality, power, nurturance, who do I want to be when I grow up, and so on. As psychoanalyst Harry Stack Sullivan once put it, "We are all more simply human than otherwise." All other principles of adult living flow from this. None make sense without it.

Men and Women
in the News

Right after I finished the first draft of the previous essay on Men and Women in Therapy, I read an article in *Seattle Weekly*. The title was "Marry Me or Move Out." In it, author Kathryn Robinson reported the stories of three women who threatened to leave the men with whom they were living unless they received a proposal of marriage. The question the article raised was, "Is there any reasonable way for a woman to get a man to make a commitment?"

At about the same time I heard a radio interview with Jane Goodall, who has studied the lives of our nearest relatives, the chimpanzees, for thirty years. She mentioned that male chimp babies are more independent of their mothers and explore more than female babies, who are more focused from the start on cultivating the relationship with mother. The tone of the conversation was that there was a lesson in this for us in our desire to understand male-female differences in our own species.

A short time later I came across an article written by a psychoanalyst, Doris Silverman, a few years ago in a back issue of one of the journals to which I subscribe. Its title was "What Are Little Girls Made Of?" Research, she argued, supports the idea that females not only have more powerful bonding tendencies than males but are better at providing secure and powerful attachments for children, so that a little of Mommy may go as far, or farther, than a lot of Daddy, and women might, therefore, be freer than men to spend time away from their children and still give them what they want and need.

So, although I do believe there is no payoff in relying on fixed and absolute gender distinctions to understand any specific human relationship, I don't believe that gender is irrelevant. Neither extreme position fits the view of things that emerges from psychotherapy. From that perspective as well as from the perspective of men and women in real relationships, there is probably no single element of human life more conflicted and confusing than gender. I think Freud saw this, and that at his best he conveyed a sense of gender and sexuality as the prime cosmic joke—as if we are being challenged to try to make something humane out of a situation in which we start with two groups whose fundamental agenda may be to use each other for as much fun, security, and profit as each can get out of the other.

Barbara Ehrenreich's 1983 book, *The Hearts of Men*, was as good an example of this, from the other side of the fence, as Davidson's arguments that I mentioned in the previous essay. American men and women emerged out of the Victorian nineteenth and into the twentieth century firmly entrenched in their roles as responsible, self-disciplined male breadwinner and revered, disempowered female consumer.

According to Ehrenreich, this was lousy, but what happened next was just as bad if not worse. Women opened their eyes and wanted out of the confinement to home, husband, and the joy of selecting the right detergent. Men opened their eyes and wanted out of "the particularly strenuous act" of traditional nose-to-the-grindstone masculinity. That sounds good, but the problem, for Ehrenreich, is that men got their freedom first. It was easier for a man to drop the old bread-winner role in favor of uncommitted, free-to-spend-on-himself bachelor—or, more to Ehrenreich's point, free-to-spend-on-himself non–alimony- and non–child-support-paying ex-husband bachelor—than it was for the average woman to escape the roles of domestic or low-paid employee.

What men were supposed to have done with the energy freed up by their liberation from unquestioning and obedient corporate drone was, in Ehrenreich's mind to, "take on more of what have been women's traditional tasks." But instead, in large numbers, once their jail door was open, they just split. Men broke their bond (or bondage to women), but women, unable, on the average, to equal male wage-earning capacity, remained bound to men. Now, however, they increasingly found themselves bound to men who were either thoughtlessly or viciously irresponsible to them.

The solution, which Ehrenreich works her way around to through a maze of other possibilities, is, ultimately, for the government to get the money from men and the corporations they control and distribute it, through income-support pro-grams, to the women who need it because they cannot get it from individual men and cannot earn it themselves, "either because they have small children to care for, or because they cannot yet find jobs that pay enough for material subsistence."

So where Davidson asks us to resign ourselves to our nineteenth-century gender roles because they represent the natural order of things, Ehrenreich suggests that we resign ourselves to a new adversarial order. These two alternatives, however, are simply lapses back into a gender obsession. Sure, it's possible to view the male characters in Robinson's story as wanting as much as they can have from women without giving anything in return, but that's not how such men have appeared to me in therapy, nor, in fact, was that how they appeared to the women in the story. These women were confused about what was happening and understood the men they were about to leave to be confused as well. The most familiar way to resolve the confusion—gender determines our fates—was the way the author finally took: Maybe there is something "inborn, so common as to seem inviolable, that makes women seek commitment where men are content without it. As a modern, thinking feminist, Anne doesn't want to believe that. Neither do Lisa or Jennifer. Neither do many of the other women I know."

But there is all this evidence arguing that it is. In addition to these three personal stories, there are the observations of Jane Goodall and the conclusions drawn from research by Doris Silverman. At first glance they add up to exactly what Davidson or Ehrenreich suggest, a chronic and irresolvable gap between naturally caring, relationship-oriented women and power-hungry, freedom-loving men. But on closer inspection they add up to something different.

When fine-tuned through the close-up perspective of therapy, the picture looks like this. Some men in therapy are unconflicted about commitment, while some resemble the characters in Robinson's cast. Yes, as Goodall suggests, girls and women seem to have a motivational tilt toward the pleasure of relationships, but boys and men know there is pleasure in them as well. More important, however, is Silverman's suggestion that women are not only more inclined toward the relational pleasures in life than the autonomous ones, but are also better at relating.

The other side of this coin is that men who appear afraid of commitment are actually men who perceive themselves as incompetent at the kind of relationship they imagine marriage involves. Perceived incompetence is a powerful psychological force in every one of our lives. We don't want to enter arenas of human interaction where we predict we will not perform adequately. It only takes the real, even if slight, edge that women may enjoy, by temperament or training or tradition, to generate all this trouble. Based solely on this slight male disadvantage in managing relationships and the emotions involved in them, many men perceive themselves as too incompetent to feel safe taking the final step up to the major leagues of lifetime relationships with women and children in marriage and family. They have been hanging on up to that point but cannot imagine going further.

None of us can. Perceived incompetence is a real barrier to growth and performance in any human domain. How it gets resolved in any particular situation is no more a fixed and universal scenario than is any specific male or female life. What is true across the board is that gender is, for all of us, the source of some perceived incompetence. Part of our collective growing up is noticing this about ourselves rather than living it out.

How Attachments Work

During the first forty years of my life, I spent a good part of the energy I had available for what is now called "male bonding" on one particular relationship. Then one day—literally, one day—that man and I found ourselves saying that what we had shared had not really been much of a friendship, that perhaps we had not ever liked each other "best" (maybe not even "a lot"), despite having "been there" for each other at various times and having talked intensely over the years. So what had we had, if not a friendship? It was, I now believe, mostly an attachment.

We all harbor two key illusions about attachments, and we tend to hold on to them despite experiences that suggest that they are not true. First, we like to believe that we will only become attached to people to whom we decide to become attached. Over the years many movies have attacked that illusion. Three that come to mind are *Kiss of the Spider Woman*;

Planes, Trains, and Automobiles; and *Rain Man*. In each one a man ended up deeply attached to another man whom he intended to exploit. There was no intention to become attached.

But merely by spending time together—in a prison cell, stuck in airports, or in a drive across the country—the two characters become attached. At one point in *Rain Man*, Charlie asks Raymond's psychiatrist if he ever spent twenty-four hours a day with Raymond for a week. When Charlie did that, he and Raymond developed feelings for each other that neither seemed capable of when they first met.

In much the same way, but without the drama of Hollywood, that man and I were thrown together in adolescence by a shared private sense of feeling ourselves to be outsiders to the larger group with whom we spent our time. That led us to spend a lot of time talking and simply being together. Nothing else was required to create a bond that felt like glue between us.

I was reminded of this when a therapy patient came to an almost identical assessment of a long-standing relationship to a woman with whom she has spent much of her adolescence and early adulthood. In one conversation that had not begun in anger (and didn't end in it) and which neither had gone into thinking of it as a moment of truth, they both found themselves saying that as much as being together had become a very comfortable habit, their relationship wasn't much of a friendship. Yet, the thought of letting go hurt. And my patient said, spontaneously, about her friend, "I am really attached to her."

This seemed to me, when I first thought of it this way, to be one of those pieces of wisdom that belonged in this book, one of those things no one ever tells you but, if you happen to discover it, really opens your eyes. Yes, you can be firmly attached to someone outside of love and friendship. There are relationships that are just attachments. And if I had any doubts about this, as I was working on this essay, I got a call from a patient who had been in analysis with me once. She was upset to have discovered that her father's second wife was, after the father's death, not interested in a relationship with her. Did she want a friendship with this woman? No. Did she want an intimate younger-woman-to-older-woman relationship? No. In fact, she felt she had been politely accepting of this woman during all the years she had known her. But she didn't have a category in mind for what existed between them, so in the absence of any feeling that it was a genuine friendship or loving bond, she assumed it was nothing emotionally meaningful at all. But now when the other woman did things that suggested she was embarking on a new life and might not want to "keep in touch," my patient found herself feeling a deep sense of loss. "I've gotten attached to her," she said. There was that word again. It's a distinct category of relationship—an attachment.

And the fact that attachments form without our intending them to, contrary to one of our illusions about them, suggests that we ought to be careful with whom we spend time. The odds are we'll start to feel attached. Once we do, we can't leave without pain. That's how attachments work.

The second common illusion about attachments overturned by these stories from life, therapy, and the movies is that we only become attached to people we like or love a lot. That too seems not to matter very much, no more than intending to get attached at all matters. Usually, we are drawn to certain people because a specific characteristic of theirs is very appealing. The fact that this characteristic—beauty, wit, some special ability, a shared history (she was my dead father's intimate partner for years)—is packaged in a human being with other characteristics we find unattractive escapes our attention during the so-called honeymoon period.

But as the relationship unfolds, we become aware of these other characteristics. Unfortunately, as we become more aware, we also become more attached, because we are spending time with that person.

Often enough, our awareness of the unappealing characteristics reaches critical mass right after we have become just enough attached so that leaving the relationship will hurt. Then we feel stuck. We still are drawn in by the qualities, but we are pushed away by other qualities we dislike. We also don't want to go through the pain of detaching, but we don't want to stay either. Many people show up in therapy right at this point, confused at the mixture of feelings.

The reason for the confusion is that the reality of how attachments work defies the illusions we harbor about them, which are really fantasies about how we would like them to work. Not only would we like it if we only became attached consciously and intentionally, but we would also like it if we only became attached to people who never disappointed us. As Annie Hall said, "If only life worked that way." But it doesn't. We get attached to many people with whom we spend a lot of time the way we get hot standing in the sun. It's what happens to human beings under those circumstances. We never like facing such uncontrollable realities. We like control, but then life happens—in this case attachments happen—and we choose from there.

Deep Talk

All therapies strive to replace our surface talk with what might be called "deep talk." In the best of all possible worlds, as we added years to our lives, we would speak more and more clearly to each other about our inner experiences. Our psychological vocabulary would increase along with our social vocabulary. That, unfortunately, is not the way life works. Instead, we come to rely on a collection of linguistic diversions that allow us to say what is on our mind without appearing to be doing so.

A college student comes home and tells his father that someone broke into his (the student's) car and stole an expensive item (belonging to the student) that was on the backseat. His father says, "You should have put it in the trunk." This sounds like advice but does not feel like advice to the student. It feels as if his father is saying, "I hate how it makes me feel when something like this happens, and I wish you would never

139

burden me with news like this." That's how it translates into deep language.

Because of how clever we all are at transforming deep talk into surface talk, we are hard to pin down. The only clues that we have to disparities between deep and surface talk are feelings that don't seem to fit with what is being said. The mother who fills her son with guilt by saying "Go and have a good time and don't worry about me" is the classic example, but almost every time we say "I only meant" or "All I said was," it's likely that we are attempting to disclaim a piece of deep talk that slipped out in our attempt to construct a well-disguised surface statement.

Another clue is uncoordinated action. A patient with whom I was working in analysis heard that at a seminar, and we agreed it contained a lot of wisdom. If we are communicating with each other, then our joint actions will be coordinated. The dance will go relatively smoothly. If the dance is not going smoothly, then, by definition, we are not communicating. And not communicating always means that our surface talk is leaving out too much deep talk for us to be able to understand each other. Too much of what we have to say is taking place in our private conversation with ourselves and too much is being left out of our out-loud conversation.

The idea from that seminar is not new in psychotherapy. Harry Stack Sullivan said it fifty years ago: Language just *appears* to be a means of communication. In most instances we use it as a cloaking device. Then, in the 1970s, building on the work of linguist Noam Chomsky, Richard Bandler and John Grinder systematized this aspect of therapy in their book *The Structure of Magic*. Neurolinguistic programming is the school of psychotherapy that emphasizes this approach most directly. But we all engage in this therapy with each other when we say something like, "You're not saying what's on your mind."

No one's surface talk reveals all his deep talk. The question is one of proportion. One way to keep the two types of talk in proper proportion is to allow more deep talk into our surface talk. That is common advice and often good advice: Make your private conversation public rather than having bits and pieces of it leak out.

Another, and less recognized, way is to talk less, to comment less often on what people around us are doing. That's much harder these days, when we have been groomed by our psychologized culture not only to live life but also annotate it with insightful commentary. Let me try an example here. From time to time a patient will ask a therapist to lie on an insurance form. The most common request I've had regards the date the treatment started. If someone started therapy with me in July and then took a new job in September, they may have to wait a year for coverage of therapy to kick in for this already ongoing treatment of a preexisting condition. Sometimes they suggest that we wait until October and submit a first insurance form on which I would state that therapy began October 1. I could offer (and did early on in my career) all sorts of reasons for not doing it (always with the implication that my doing so would be bad for the therapy) and all sorts of interpretations of what else (besides money) might have motivated the patient to make the request. But the best response, for me, has turned out to be "I don't do that."

There's a difference between not saying what's on your mind because you're afraid or because you don't think you're competent enough emotionally or interpersonally to manage the rest of the conversation that would follow, and not saying what's on your mind because saying it would just be a way of saying "I want you to like my decision because it's thoughtful and psychologically grounded." Talk is not useful just because it's deep.

After I've said that I don't lie on insurance forms, there really is not anything else useful for me to say on that subject. Requests for explanations are really covert attempts to reopen the conversation. To respond to them is to communicate that I am open to further discussion of the topic. But I'm not. To say anything further would be simply to make excuses for my unwillingness to be more cooperative in the other person's pursuit of the agenda of getting reimbursed.

Deep talk is often a disguised way of offering excuses. "I want you to view my verbal attack on you this morning as a reflection of the distress of my divorce and, therefore, as deep talk (a good thing). I was sharing my innermost emotional state with you when I attacked you." We may offer that type of deep-talk excuse because we genuinely believe it's the most useful thing to say. It isn't. The most useful thing to say is that you don't have anything useful to say about what you did beyond that you now regret it—if, of course, you regret it—and that you want to open up a new conversation now. The evidence that deep talk has been useful is not that you feel relieved but that your subsequent interactions with the other person are better, smoother, more productive, better coordinated.

Men and Their Power

It's a twentieth-century cliché to observe that we all have a masculine and a feminine side. The definitions of the feminine part that I have heard over the years from both men and women usually have something to do with caring and relationships. The masculine part, by contrast, is usually characterized by a fascination with power and control.

But the best description of "the masculine" that I've heard came from a woman who said, "It's the part of me that protects me." Masculinity is protective power. But whom is it intended to protect, and from what? It is intended to protect all of us from intimidation. It is for me a commitment not to control others by verbal, emotional, or physical intimidation as well as a commitment to do everything I can to prevent anyone else from controlling me, or anyone about whom I care, in any of those ways. It is, by definition, the same for each of us.

If children have been exposed to this healthy masculine impulse in one or both of their parents, they are likely to emerge into adolescence with an awareness that their lives among their peers are filled with possibilities for intimidation. This doesn't lead to paranoia but to protective caring toward themselves and others. You can see instances in which they show that they have acquired the ability to say, "I just don't do that, even if the decision not to do it carries with it the threat of intimidation by you." And, conversely, you can see them decline the opportunity to intimidate or humiliate others as a way to control a situation. They don't have to think this through time after time. It becomes a value that has a life of its own.

We seem to have a tough time getting this straight. For a couple of millennia we treated this masculine protective power as if it were the sole province of men, as if it were a gender-related characteristic. And if you treat something that way, then it often becomes that. I don't know who started this tradition of men having sole access to masculine power and women having sole access to feminine caring, and I don't believe theorists who claim to know. It was a lousy tradition, and it didn't work. Kept alive solely in the hands of men, it deteriorated into a bizarre version of itself in which only a few incredibly violent but well-intentioned guys could protect all the rest of us from equally violent but malevolent guys.

Then there was a time, beginning somewhere in the sixties, where we all seemed to think it was a good idea to throw out this quintessential component of the psychologically masculine. Since it had become so perverse anyway, it seemed as though we should rid ourselves of it. Men, especially, seemed to think women wanted them to rid themselves of this traditional masculine stuff. I'm not sure that was ever true. In any case the idea of men abandoning their masculine power in favor of feminine caring seems to have had a short life in the desires of both men and women.

An increasing number of men who were not exposed to this protective masculine piece of human nature during their childhood are finding it, and embracing it enthusiastically, in the novels of writers such as Tom McGuane and Richard Ford as well as in the detective series created by writers like Robert Parker and Richard Hoyt. Men have shown as much of an interest in the personal lives of these authors as in the lives of their characters. They find through them access to a vision of masculine power that had been hidden.

But it would be a repetition of the same old mistake if we simply reinvoked the idea that masculine protective power is the sole province of men. It is, I suspect, one of those gender-tilted qualities. It may be a little easier for a lower voice and a larger body to successfully counter certain instances of abusive attempts at intimidation, but everyone can embrace such protective power as a piece of their humanity and as a value to be lived.

To the delight of the gender–minimizer in me, the useful-tough quality of the male characters invented by writers like McGuane and Parker is showing up in women invented by writers like Sue Grafton and Sara Paretsky. Grafton's Kinsey Millhone and Paretsky's V. I. Warshawski are tough but humane characters just like Parker's Spenser, who—like anyone you or I would want around in a situation where the threat of intimidation existed—can blend wisecracking humor, emotional awareness, and genuine tough grit into a protective psychological power that works.

If this trend in literature forecasts a rescue of masculine protective power from both its perversely exaggerated and ridiculously disempowered forms, and also forecasts an embracing of it by both men and women, then masculine power will finally have come home.

The Bringer of Joy

Recently, I attended a seminar in which current research about parents and their adolescent children was reviewed. We enlightened and liberated parents of the 1990s, it turns out—both mothers and fathers—have an interesting but not too enlightened habit. We consistently tell our sons to work hard and strive to be the best at what they do because it's a tough, competitive world out there. Then we look tenderly at our daughters and say, "Don't worry, just be happy." Adolescents report this difference, and researchers observe it.

I've wondered what sort of underlying fantasy about males and females haunts our cultural unconscious with enough force to keep us doing this even when many women are choosing careers as competitive as those pursued by their brothers. Then I came across an essay on female psychology that started out with an interesting and innovative interpretation of the ancient myth of Amor and Psyche, but ended with the startlingly archaic message that the role of women is to bring joy, ecstasy, and pleasure into our lives.

Men, the author argued, value women because women are the bearers of joy, and therefore, he implied, men rightly expect women to provide such joy. There's a hint thrown in that men have a female side from which they might also derive some of this ecstatic joy, but it was clear to me that the main message was for women to accept this role and get on with providing more good old-fashioned joy than they are now doing.

If most of us are consciously or unconsciously harboring that notion about women, it would certainly help to explain why parents are still telling their girls to be happy. The message might more clearly be stated as, "We're all depending on you to be happy, and in turn to bring happiness into the lives of the men and children around you. So don't get too wrapped up in heroic ventures. Leave those for your brother."

This brings back to mind a story a friend told me. Plans were being made to organize a study group in his graduate-school class, and someone suggested that he become the leader because he was the smartest guy in the class. He had the presence of mind immediately to say he didn't want that label draped over him because then he would have to live up to it for the rest of the time the group was together.

It strikes me that adolescent girls ought to be saying the same thing: "Thanks, but no thanks. That sounds like a nice job, but I'll pass for this lifetime. Let Johnny be the bringer of joy. I'll watch."

I'm not arguing for all of us to tell each other to take care of your own happiness because we don't care about anyone but ourselves. But women have enough of a natural focus on relationships without us having to groom them further for the job by sending the message to adolescent girls that they must take responsibility for being the bearers of joy and ecstasy. There is no doubt, however, that we—men and women together—have agreed that this is their job.

As often happens, as I was thinking about this idea, I came across a unique analysis of women in literature that further confirmed its validity. In *Seduction and Betrayal* Elizabeth Hardwick put it this way: If the life of a heroine in a novel revolves around a sexual betrayal that she commits, it makes a difference to most readers whether she is the central female character in the story or a helpless female "victim" at the edge of the story. A real heroine has to be pure and innocent at heart, despite some piece of behavior to the contrary, if she is to carry the story. This innocence is "not physical innocence, but a lack of mean calculations, of vindictiveness, of self-abasing weakness." The version of this sentiment that I observe most often in the real world—even in the comments of both male and female therapists during discussions of therapy cases—is the common opinion that unhappy men are depressed while unhappy women are bitchy.

We have been training our sons and daughters in these roles of autonomous-man-of-action and woman-who-cares-and-brings-joy for so long that trying to figure out now how much of contemporary male or female identity is wired-in is a futile effort. Neither biology nor universal social necessity can be distinguished from a multithousand-year-old habit. Habits form and stick even when they are maladaptive and life-robbing. The argument that the way to break this habit is to establish that women's approach to life is authentic is, in my view, more of the same overgenderizing. Every national, racial, ethnic, or gender-derived approach to life is authentic. The ideal that therapy promotes is for each individual to be able to develop an identity that expresses his or her unique coming-into-the-world. I don't want my daughters to have to choose, on the basis of society's or sociologists' mandate, between power and objectification (the alleged male agenda) or caring and joyful relating. And I certainly don't want either of them, if they turned out not to be wonderfully gifted at relating, to feel deficient as women. I want them to grow as far in either or both of these directions as their own unique joy for life leads them.

And what about our sons, who are now caught in male biology or an old male habit of not paying enough attention to relationships? How about, my wife suggested when I asked her about this, if we just tell adolescent boys who don't seem to notice it on their own that it might be worth their time to learn something about how to establish joyful relationships with women and with children. That appeals to me. It captures the brand of wisdom about life I associate with good therapy. I wish more men told that to more boys starting right now—that their chance for a happy life depends just as much on knowing how to be happy with women and children as it does on money and status. I wish someone had told me that twenty-five years ago. I didn't like learning it the hard way.

How Young Men and
Women Become
Middle-Aged

Like most of the people I've met inside and outside of psychotherapy, I spent most of my twenties and thirties feeling trapped
in a struggle with the world. There were forces holding me
down and holding me back, keeping me pinned to the mat.
One day shortly before my fortieth birthday, it occurred to me
that this whole sense of struggle had been a projection of my
version of the narcissism of adolescence and young adulthood.

For all those years no one would have been able to convince
me that life was just happening, with me moving around
inside it, experiencing my share of spiritual and material suc-
cesses and failures. From my perspective life was personally
involved with me, and, more specifically, it was pushing
against me. "Youth has an agenda," as Frank Conroy has
captured this feeling, "that . . . the world is a battleground,
with hostile geography hiding hostile forces that must be over-
come."

Then one day my perspective shifted dramatically. I still don't know exactly how or why, but it did.

All of a sudden, life was just there. The rest of the human race was just going about its business. You know those scenes where one character is kicking and banging at a door to open it and the other character turns the knob and the door opens. It was never locked. No one was holding it closed on the other side. Similarly, my *self* was not in a struggle with anyone.

This lifting of the fog of first-half-of-life self-absorption, Conroy wrote, "can come as a profound relief, because it is no longer necessary to spend so much energy shoring up the self, and because the world emerges as a sweeter place through which to move."

I have never seen the process accelerated by any type of therapy or counseling. The new feeling just appears one day, and from that point on you start to feel that you can just do what you do and it will be more or less okay with everybody. And you wonder what younger people find so urgent about getting the right job or getting into the right graduate school or whatever rites of passage haunt the young people in your part of the world. Those feelings seem far away.

That, unfortunately, leaves young people alone with those feelings, without much connection to the generations that have come out on the other side of the struggle. Many of us move through it alone, feeling that only through strenuous and constant self-assertion will we gain a foothold in life. When the day comes that we suddenly feel we have achieved firm footing on level ground rather than hanging on to a slim ledge looking up at the top, there is a sigh of relief. If it hasn't happened yet, wait. It happens.

PART FOUR

WORK, ACHIEVEMENT, AND MONEY

Turning Play into Work and Work into Madness

A long time ago I read an interview with Rod Serling, creator of *The Twilight Zone*. Writing scripts for the show started out as a pleasurable activity for him. He wrote them because it was what he wanted to do.

Then he started getting paid enormous sums of money for each week's show—fifty thousand dollars, if I am remembering the interview exactly. That's a seemingly happy combination, getting paid a lot of money for doing what you like. The money had the opposite effect, however, leaving Serling feeling the network owned him and that he now worked for the money, not for the joy of it. He couldn't stop. He wanted the money.

Years later in graduate school I came across a set of interesting findings in social psychology that suggest that this phenomenon is common. If we start out doing something because it is intrinsically appealing to us and then we get significant tangible rewards for doing it, we start to feel as though we are performing for the rewards, and the activity becomes less enjoyable.

A group of psychologists went into a nursery school and selected children who spontaneously chose to play with colored markers. They were doing it because it was fun for them. The psychologists picked out some of these children and promised them that they would get money for coloring with the markers. As promised, when they played with the markers, they got paid. Another group was given the same reward when they played with the markers, but they were not told ahead of time they would get it. The final group of original spontaneous players was left alone.

The children who knew they would get something for playing spent just enough time with the markers to meet the requirement for getting paid; that is, they quickly became jaded workers. The group that was left alone kept spending significant amounts of time playing with the markers as they had previously. The children who were rewarded unexpectedly, however, started spending more time coloring. It's apparently one thing to be doing what you enjoy and then to have someone come along and say, "That's nice; here's a reward," and quite a different experience to have someone tell you that if you do something, you'll get paid for it.

It also turns out that watching people—children or adults—play can make the playing less enjoyable, if the feeling is one of being under surveillance. That feels like external pressure, in the same way that getting paid does. So, some social psychologists have concluded that maybe teachers are not doing students a favor by setting up a system of rewards for good performance. And maybe parents should give rewards unexpectedly for a job well done rather than arranging things ahead of time.

This, however, is not a phenomenon only of childhood. It is not simply something that adults do or don't do to children. It is also something adults do to each other and to themselves.

One prediction that follows logically from this theory would be that many of us who seem best adjusted to the contemporary workplace may actually be suffering the most. And this is precisely what Douglas LaBier found in his ground-breaking seven-year study of the lives of professionals between the ages of twenty-five and forty-seven. The results of his study were reported in a fascinating book called *Modern Madness: The Emotional Fallout of Success*, which I had the opportunity to review when it was published in 1986.

My own interpretation of what he found was that too few of us stop and ask why we are doing what we are doing. Right from the start of our adult work lives, that question should be primary. There has to be some positive answer in addition to money.

The longer the asking of the question is delayed, the harder it becomes to face it squarely, answer it honestly, and see any way out. In the movie *Da* the main character was offered a job by a local businessman and decided to take it while waiting for the door to open to what he really wanted to do. The owner warned him that this job wasn't likely to be very satisfying—not really up his alley—but the young man responded that he knew that and wasn't worried because they both knew he didn't intend to make a career out of it. "Don't be so sure," the older man cautioned. "A job is like a lobster pot. It's a lot easier to get into one than it is to get out."

A significant number of patients end up telling me—often while believing that their dilemma is more complex—that they are simply unable to live with any real measure of satisfaction while working at their present job. They usually don't want that to be the answer, because they have constructed a life with that job or career as a cornerstone, and they fear that the whole structure will fall apart if they pull out that piece.

As understandable as this attitude is, sometimes it feels to me as if they are no different from people who tell their physician that they can't breathe too well anymore, and then don't like it when they hear that they can't smoke and breathe in the same lifetime. It is torturous for some people to give up smoking, and it is torturous for some people to change careers or jobs. Often, however, it appears that they cannot "breathe" emotionally and live with any dignity while continuing to engage in that activity forty or fifty hours per week. As impossible as it seems, something must change.

What can an adult do in that kind of trap? One strategy is to take all your complaints and synthesize them into one wish for change—a change in your pattern of activity at work that you can describe in a few sentences to whoever has the power to effect such a change. It's not enough to have the will to make things better for yourself. You must also formulate a clear and individualized wish and tell it to someone who can help you create the change.

A more radical alternative suggested by LaBier for an adult who has decided to stay in a job that isn't satisfying is to accept the fact that the job will no longer satisfy you and to look outside work for some of the good feelings you once thought would come from work. Do something else "with seriousness, discipline, study, and commitment."

Then, I'd add, start telling yourself that that's what you do. I can recall when I drove a taxi in New York City for a while that half the people in the garage identified themselves as ballet dancers or writers or musicians or artists. "Oh, I write novels. Nobody buys them yet, and maybe nobody will. But that's what I do. To pay the bills, I drive a cab, but I'm not a cabdriver."

That's how I now hear, in my memory, what they were saying, and I can see how it helped them to stay sane. Most of us feel funny saying that because it feels phony. Other people always assume we mean that we make a significant amount of money at what we say we do, so they want to know which galleries we've shown our paintings in or who publishes our books and articles. Then we feel silly saying that at the moment we write for ourselves and our family or that our paintings are all shown in our home and the homes of our friends.

The other person, as if determined to confirm our worry that we are being silly or pretentious or phony, invariably says, "Oh, you paint as a hobby. But what do you do?" The answer should still be that you paint or write for your life, but for money you work as an attorney or a cabdriver. If you do it with seriousness, discipline, study, and commitment, then it's what you do. Own it.

The bottom line is that what you are doing is never the only thing you might be doing. The status quo is never all there is, but it is what you know. Contemplating change often means considering a plunge into the darkness. We all fear falling on our faces, but some of us move into the dark anyway, even if it's a small step at a time.

Just Because You're
Good at It

I remember reading a short story about a college student who mastered throwing the javelin. It was a spiritual as well as physical activity for him, but no one else understood that. Ultimately, one of his throws went farther than anything on record. His friend who had been working with him throughout his training assumed he would be headed for the Olympic trials, but exactly the opposite happened. He said he was finished throwing. He had found meaning in attaining mastery of the javelin. Now he had done that, and the activity had no further meaning for him. He had never intended to compete. "But," his bewildered friend argued, "you're great at it. You're the best. You could have an Olympic Gold Medal." The athlete just shrugged.

Listening to a young woman in therapy brought this story back to mind. She had spent most of her childhood completely devoted to mastering a musical instrument. She was extraordinarily talented and committed. Teachers wanted to work with her, summer festival schools offered her scholarships, and eventually orchestras invited her to play with them. When she suddenly decided to stop accepting these invitations and instead to use the money she had earned to open a travel agency, her family pushed her into analysis. She was, as you might have imagined, viewed as crazy for throwing away a career she had so painstakingly built, and which was now just starting to really pay off.

What I'm supposed to do as an analyst is listen for conflict in such a scenario. The obvious place to look in a scenario like this is conflict over success. And it was certainly there: conflict over how clearly her fame and fortune highlighted her mother's belief that her own life lacked it; conflict over the angry and envious components of her competitiveness; and conflict over a fear she both experienced and resented that such a career might preclude romance and family. But there was also an increasingly clear conviction that what she sought most in playing at this point was admiration. She was no longer in it for the joy of mastery and the pleasure of music. She craved the admiration, but after a while it had started not to be enough. The pleasure of being admired for doing something so well just wasn't sustaining. What she felt at first was simply the loss of motivation to keep playing. But that had, from the start, reflected the waning of the power of being admired to keep her engaged in her career. As it became clear that to continue playing music would, for her, have been mostly a pursuit of admiration and a pursuit purchased with all her available time and energy, her conviction that she wanted a change increased (much to the dismay of her parents, who will probably never push anyone into analysis again, at least not with me).

Being good at something and being admired for it usually go

hand in hand. The feeling of being admired is powerfully seductive but rarely sustaining. Children can drive themselves into a frenzy to keep it coming once they've had a taste. It's simply not possible to create out of this one ingredient the kind of career that can be fit into a genuine adulthood. The taste is too overpowering.

Doing and Having

I wanted to write this book when I was twenty-seven and had just finished my basic training in clinical psychology. I wanted to be paid large sums of money ahead of time by some publisher so I would be free to write without anxiety or deprivation. I just could never think of anything useful to say. I resented the fact that the world was such a place that this small detail would keep publishers from subsidizing my writing career. If only someone would subsidize me, then the available time and peace of mind would certainly free my creative potential, and useful stuff would come pouring out of my fingertips onto those blank pages. I was sure of that. But the world kept demanding I carve out my own time and space to be passionately creative. I hated that.

The conflict between passion and money is one that emerges in many of our conversations, including those between therapists and patients. Many of us are profoundly upset at the refusal of the world to let us do what we want and, at the same time, give us as much money as we want for doing it. This conflict between doing and having is irresolvable for some of us. It haunts us throughout life.

A not-uncommon reaction is to imply that the problem is with society. Our "screwed-up" middle-class, bourgeois society makes us choose between money and passion. A terrific and passionately committed schoolteacher, the antibourgeois argument goes, should make more than a lawyer who spends all day getting major traffic violations reduced to lesser ones, but our perverse values keep it from working that way in the real world.

A patient of mine took this complaint against bourgeois society to one of its extremes and developed his own theory that the people who get paid the most are the ones who do things that seem to triumph over the harsh realities of life. Physicians give us the hope that we can transcend pain and death, lawyers the promise of justice (often in the form of monetary compensation for random bad things that happen to us), and athletes the illusion that we can play forever. Poorly paid people, on the other hand, my patient's argument went, do jobs that remind us life is really tough. Teachers, for example, are just reminders that life is hard work, that not everyone is equally equipped to learn quickly and efficiently, and that children are a burden as well as a joy to have around. There's never going to be much money in that.

In her January 1991 *Atlantic Monthly* essay, Suzanne Gordon took to another extreme this argument that the way we pay people in various jobs reflects a perverse social system. Our bourgeois market society forces us to choose between money and the natural tendency we would all have—if it weren't for the power of the market—to spend less time earning and more time caring. That's the argument she started with anyway.

Soon, however, she was into the same type of gender argument as the one Barbara Ehrenreich used years ago. Only women have the natural tendency to care more about other people than about success and money. Men will have to be forced into it by rules or laws that limit how many hours they can work and by government redistribution of money to women in various ways. Finally, however, she updated Ehrenreich's argument for the 1990s. Women had let us all down too. Once they got the opportunity, they too were often choosing success and money over caring for children and the elderly. She made an appeasing argument to her female readers that they were being *forced* into this, while men are natural market slaves, but her point was clear. The seductions of the market were proving too powerful even for allegedly naturally caring women. They too were drifting out of caring activities and into money-making ones. They were no longer becoming teachers and nurses, and so we have shortages in these professions. They would really want to do these things if they weren't penalized financially for it. But apparently men would not want to do these caring things at any price. So men were choosing to abandon caring, and women were being forced to abandon it, and they all need to be forced back into it.

There are explanations of pay differences between professions that are less supportive of an attack on bourgeois, middle-class life than Gordon's explanations. Maybe we are all stuck with various imperfect solutions to the problem of trying to balance doing what we want and having what we want. Maybe many of us believe getting money for ourselves, our children, and our elderly parents is one way of caring for us and them. Maybe not having enough money scares the hell out of us more than not having enough caring. Maybe we are all inclined to pay others as little as we can get away with paying them while trying to get others to pay us as much as we think we can get from them. Maybe caring for others in the way Gordon defines caring is just one thing among many that human beings like to do, and not enough of us want to do enough caring to suit her—and maybe, therefore, the point she ends up with at the end of her essay is simply the only point she could have ended up with: that when women got the chance to do things besides caring for others as a full-time job, many of them chose these other things, angering Gordon in the process.

In therapy many angry fantasies about how the world is cheating us out of being caring, carefree, passionately creative, and financially secure—all at the same time—fall apart. Patients often see in their own private version of that angry complaint against society the frustrated desire many of us share to be paid lots of money to play with our passions—a desire frustrated by one of life's big realities: Other people want to keep their money and will usually only give it to us if they are persuaded that doing so will be of direct and personal benefit to them. Accepting that means accepting that often in life we must decide between doing what we want and having what we want. And coming to terms with this in some way is one of the major hurdles between adolescence and adulthood.

The Cost of Things

You don't really pay for things with money. You pay for them with time. "In five years, I'll have put enough away to buy that vacation house we want. Then I'll slow down or get out of this business altogether." Okay, that means the house will cost you five years—five out of eighty, maybe. That's one sixteenth of your whole life; one twelfth of your adult life; one quarter of the time you'll spend living with any one of your children.

I've read a number of interviews over the years in which a husband and father, in changing careers to spend more time with his family, said he had never heard of a man on his deathbed who wished he had spent more time at the office. Translate the dollar value of the car or the house or anything else into time, and then see if it's still worth it.

This is not a diatribe against materialism. I think human beings are acquisitive by nature, not by perversion as some social critics have argued. If there is something out there that is useful, or novel, or stimulating in some way, people want it. Generally, everything that exists sooner or later turns out to be desirable to someone.

Sometimes, however, you can't do what you want and have what you want at once because each requires a different expenditure of time. Those are the moments when you have to think of the cost of the thing in terms of time and not dollars. Dan O'Brien published his first novel, *The Spirit of the Hills*, when he was forty. During his previous twenty years he wrote, but not with much financial success. So there must have been things he wanted to have along the way and couldn't have because he was doing what he wanted. There is, however, no way he could have worked as an attorney during his twenties and thirties, then sat down and wrote *The Spirit of the Hills*. That book was written by someone who had been at it for a while—someone who had been *spending* his time writing.

You see, that phrase *spending your time* is not a metaphor. It's how life works.

There Should Be More

"The deepest feeling of all is that there should be more." And the more we get, the more emphatically this feeling seems to grip us. In the novel *Vestments*, Sebastian Taggart already has the three big pieces of the younger male baby boomer's "good life." He lives with a "classy" woman. They share an "elegant" apartment in a desirable neighborhood of Cambridge, Massachusetts. And he has one of the "hot" jobs as an editorial writer for a Boston television station. "But," as the book jacket summarizes it to resonate with the same desire in many of us, "he wants more," and in pursuit of more, he dresses as a priest when he visits his dying, senile, very Catholic aunt who might disinherit him from her fortune if he doesn't play out her fantasy that he became the priest she wanted him to be.

Maybe it's in our not-so-highly-evolved genes. In one study monkeys were given tokens that they could insert in slots to get food and water, but once they discovered that the tokens had value, they began to hoard them and had to be rescued from starving themselves. Maybe they were saving up for their own apartment in Cambridge. In any case the behavior is familiar.

Borrowing the most powerful techniques from psychology, the marketers and advertisers are able to keep our desires and expectations one step ahead of our ability to acquire. In fact, the evidence from satisfaction surveys strongly suggests that they are increasing the distance between what they can make us want and what we can have, so that we feel more and more dissatisfied as the decades go on.

Psychologist Paul Wachtel calls this *the poverty of affluence*. The craziness of it is that some of our children will grow up and manipulate the desires of the others and will, of course, be manipulated in turn. We are raising the next generation of frustrated consumers (who may face house prices double or triple what they are today) on a steady diet of television ads that get partially satisfied every Christmas and birthday.

Most children have fantasies of desire long before they have fantasies of accomplishment. Third-graders can tell you what kind of car they want to drive while not having much of an idea of what kinds of relationships they might like to have or what kind of work they might like to do. Each generation becomes more like those monkeys than the one before it. We may be going backward, and if we are, then what is most likely fueling that regression is the deep feeling that there should be more—a notion offered by one of Jim Harrison's characters in his novel *Sundog*. If we all are born believing there should be more than there is, then we are ready-made for each other's manipulations.

When our kids see all the new toys and junk foods on television, it complements their belief that there should be more and here comes some of it right into their living room via the magic box. We may need courses for elementary schoolchildren titled "What There Is." There is love and work and the land and books and play and food and clothing and shelter, but there are not talking dolls that cost a hundred dollars. Somebody just made that up.

Another character in *Sundog* has an answer for the first one: "There *is* a lot more. You just can't see it from anywhere you bother looking." That's what drove those monkeys crazy. I don't want it to get my kids, but I'm not sure I can stop it.

Net Worth

This topic frightens me. I got the title from the movie *Wall Street*. Playing a highly successful but low-on-integrity investor, Michael Douglas tells Charlie Sheen that 1 percent of the population owns 50 percent of America and that 90 percent of us have no net worth. Net worth. I never heard that expression once in school. When did it become important?

In the sixties I was convinced that the net worth that mattered was spiritual and psychological net worth. Now I am told that the reason I could feel that way was because my parents, like most people in the period after the Second World War, found it sufficiently easy to accumulate net worth that it spilled over easily into my life. I thought it was a given.

Then after college I discovered it wasn't, that it was hard to get, that even my parents didn't have as much of it as they seemed to and that when you don't have it and people who do have it are made constantly visible to you by *Money* magazine and the daily CNN News financial report, then you want it. You can feel sick about not having it and not knowing how to get it. But I believe that 90 percent of us don't have it to any significant degree, while a few of us have a lot of it.

Having grown up in a working-class family and now living in a world of professionals, I feel as though I'm on a fence. In the working-class view of the world that I knew as a child, being well-off meant having "a buck in your pocket." And as often as not, the pleasure of that buck came from spending it. Now the physicians and psychologists and psychoanalysts and lawyers that I know talk often about equity and funds and retirement accounts—net worth.

I think that most of them have more of it than I do. Sometimes I get the feeling that they think I have more of it than they do. I'll never know. They'll never know. People, including patients in analysis, will reveal their sexual fantasies more easily than their net worth. It's a taboo that even the most persistent therapist accepts. We hardly ever get a clear picture of the financial status of our patients, even while learning every other secret in their lives. It's the most personal thing about them.

I don't even know whether I think that wanting to have net worth is sane or crazy. I know it can scare me to think I don't have enough of if. When the IRS wants taxes and my daughter's college sends a letter about the tuition increase for next year, and all of us need medical and dental care at the same time, and, of course, our medical insurance only pays half after a large deductible or doesn't cover those particular services at all—then I feel scared. I guess what I'm feeling is the shortage of net worth.

Then, on the other hand, I can step back and think that maybe the 90 percent of us with little or no net worth have it right. What's important is being loving and generous and spiritually fulfilled. But that's too simple a dichotomy. That's left over from elementary school religion classes. The first shall be last and the last shall be first. The rich man is a spiritual pervert. I don't really believe that anymore. What do I believe about money? I don't know. As for my patients, that's the hardest part of me for me to know.

How much should I try to get and how hard should I try to get it? At one minute I envy those childless couples in *Money* magazine, who, in their thirties, are wondering where to invest the $100,000 they accumulated in their money-market account while working as merchant marines or forest rangers or stockbrokers. Then, later, I don't.

Are they really living when they are sitting around playing with their money and wondering which vintage to stock in their wine cellar and which rental property to buy next? Maybe they are. In the sixties I mocked them. Now maybe I am them, or maybe when I think I'm not, I want to be.

And then I hear that people with real net worth are not those people in the magazines at all. They are just kidding themselves. They think the good life is flying first class.

The people with real net worth inherited it from their parents, and it's too late to get in, except for a small handful of lucky and clever newcomers who, in each generation, will catapult their family out of the struggle and into the secure inner circle of enough permanent net worth to cover the expenses of the next ten generations without anybody doing anything but picking up the interest and dividend checks from the mailbox.

I think this business of net worth is all around us and has always been. As soon as one person in the group starts to show an interest in power, starts to see how it works, and starts to use it to control the group and get what he or she wants, then everyone will start to use it. No one has any choice anymore.

Adults know that and accept it even if they don't like it. Power exists, and we all have to make decisions about how to deal with it.

Thinking of that leads me to imagine a group of my ancestors sitting around and going out every day for a few hours to gather grain and seeds and nuts. And then someone gets the idea to gather extra and keep it for himself. And then one day he goes up to someone and says, Hey, I don't feel like making myself a new cloak. And besides, you're the best cloak-maker in the group. Stay home this morning. Don't go out and gather grain. It's raining anyway. Stay here in your cave and make me a cloak, and I'll give you the food you would have gathered.

If that works, the next step may be, Hey, I've always envied your cave, up here on the hill with a view of the river. I've been saving some food for a year or two. Let me have your cave, and I'll give you enough grain so you won't have to get up and go out and gather anything for months. You can live in my old cave and, let's say, what the hell, just give me a pound of grain for every day you stay there. We'll call it rent.

And so it started. Only my ancestor was the renter and somebody else's was the landlord. And I'm trying to figure out how to cross the line and become one of the net-worthers. I wish my grandfather or great-grandfather had done it. Easier for me.

I remember the moment when my father realized that I worked by the hour just as he had when he was painting apartments in New York City and I could hear some disappointment in his voice. I guess he thought all that education would get me out of the loop. I'd get to the point where I just had a lot of money without actually having to work for it.

In Arthur Miller's short story "The Misfits," later made into a movie, the two men are out on the range talking, and they agree that no matter how bad it gets out there, it beats "wages."

Wages. Do I work for wages? I guess in that conversation with my father, it occurred to him that I do. Just that he got his from one employer at a time and I hire myself out to ten or twenty employers at a time for one to five hours a week each at a set hourly wage. The alternative, the only alternative, as Miller's free-lance cowboys saw it, was to get something someone else wanted and then sell it to him. They got wild horses out on the range.

This occupation let them exercise a fair amount of self-direction, or at least in some sense they experienced it that way. So it seems to them to be the way to go. Maybe I do that too. I get money from patients. If I can get a little more than I and my family can spend, then I can sell the extra money to a fund manager for interest and dividends. After a while I may have net worth, self-worth, self-esteem, the envy of others, my portfolio in *Money*, a man with a lot of stuff, enough stuff to last a lifetime, two lifetimes. I'm sick with excitement.

PART FIVE

FINAL THOUGHTS

Where the Sixties Went

"Where does the time go?" Usually, when that question gets asked, no one tries to answer it. But in one comedy routine a character replied, "Cleveland." Somehow it seemed right.

Many of us alive today came of age in the sixties, and the answer to the title question of this essay touches on our ability to grow up. Adolescence is always hard to get past, but when the age of your adolescence has been encapsulated as a unique moment in time, it's even harder. Did we digest and metabolize the sixties into something stable and lasting? Or did we spit it out and move on?

Like the person who asked where time goes, most of us experience confusion when we are asked where the sixties went. Every generation forms a group identity, and then, years later, wonders what happened to its values.

If we had been asked, right in the middle of the sixties, to guess where our adolescent fantasies of how life should be lived would most likely go and with whom they would survive, we probably would have picked Haight-Ashbury or Boulder, or Greenwich Village. But you can't find that piece of the psychology of the baby-boom generation in any of those places. And we would probably have guessed that some group such as the English lit majors would have kept it alive, but most of them have been assimilated into university bureaucracies where they argue about the deconstruction of the novel.

It may, however, turn out that at least one large slice of those adolescent fantasies is alive and well in the economy of southern California. It takes a few twists and turns to get from the ideals of the sixties to the glitz of L.A., so bear with me on this.

First off, I'm not sure how well I remember the sixties. After having read a hundred essays on the years between 1964 and 1972, I can't tell if the images in my mind are composites of those reports or actual memories. And I'm suspicious of people my age who seem to have been taking notes on their youth while living through it. I'm not sure you can do both at the same time. Freud strongly discouraged analysts from trying to take notes and listen to patients simultaneously. It seems as though it ought to be at least as difficult to take notes and live through an entire period of history with full attention to what's going on. Someone argued recently that if you remember too much detail from the sixties, maybe you weren't there. I don't know.

One thing is certain. Every generation of adolescents has a collective fantasy about how their lives as adults will compare with adult lives of people in their parents' generation. During modern times, up until the sixties, that fantasy usually included having a bigger piece of the rock. In the sixties this got turned upside down, and the fantasy was better living through having and needing less. It was a gamble, and for the most part it did not pay off. The gamble was that our collective psyche could make that adjustment, that we could develop a taste for smaller and more self-contained living, that we would, could somehow regulate ourselves into being less expansive than previous generations.

The other two major parts of the fantasy of the sixties depended on our being able to make this psychic adjustment. One was our imagining that we could transform society from a win-lose into a win-win arrangement. Competition was the enemy in the sixties. "Upwardly mobile" was a profanity. Having found some way to be happy with less, we would not need to climb over each other, as we imagined our parents were trying to do, in a hierarchical perversion of communal spirit. We wanted everyone—regardless of race, gender, or talent—to be able to share in the good times.

But in the early seventies the Arabs shrank the good times beyond our tolerance for win-win. And maybe our government did something not so helpful in response. I can't remember now. I didn't read the business section of the daily paper then. Anyway, whatever it was, there was no way we could have predicted that the size of the rock would shrink so much when we were imagining how we would not compete with each other for pieces of it.

In a way that seems very odd to me now, one part of the adolescent fantasy of the sixties does seem to have weathered the storm and made it into the adult psyches of the eighties and nineties. And I found it reflected in a place I would never have imagined would turn out to be the repository of a sixties fantasy—the business world of southern California.

As one report captured it, in a discussion of why Los Angeles was replacing New York City as the economic capital of the country: "Los Angeles may emerge as the prototype of a new kind of American metropolis—one that seeks its sustenance not from entrenched institutions, but from the entrepreneurial verve, work ethic, and creativity of its people." A man I know who wanted to be a presidential adviser develops—out of his house-office in the Hollywood hills—ideas for major real estate development projects that always have some potential to improve the quality of life in the area for which they are intended. He didn't make it into politics, but he gambles his time and energy on the possibility of making places different in big ways and affecting people's lives in ways he values, and it may turn out that this was what he was after all along.

Learning to feed less off entrenched institutions was certainly the third key part of that sixties adolescent fantasy—with a healthy dose of creativity thrown in. (That a work ethic of any kind would have been a necessary ingredient in this stew may be something only a business major would have guessed in the sixties.)

The fact that this part of the fantasy might have survived best among the business majors rather than the English lit students and writers, for example, many of whom seem to have run themselves into a huddled and esoteric mass within academia, is certainly a surprise to me. A good twist in the plot. Something Shakespeare might have thrown in at the end to remind us to laugh at ourselves.

But maybe we shouldn't be so surprised. Despite the attention given lately to our inner child and the need to be playful and childlike, adulthood is not simply an extension of childhood, and you're not automatically an adult because you have healed the wounds inflicted on you as a child. Adulthood is a different business altogether, as I have argued in a variety of ways throughout this book. But it is a business, essentially the business—as I guess I'd like to sum it up now—of the unavoidable. Any basic human concern that you have avoided until now will return to stare you down. You didn't learn to enjoy and manage sexual relationships. Doesn't matter. You'll either figure it out or be tormented by not having done so. You don't know what you want to do about making a buck. Ignorance of adulthood is no excuse. You'll end up doing something anyway. It was big-time denial for us to have thought we'd all just do what we wanted and the money would be there. Only the business majors knew that in 1968.

The business majors? L.A. Entrepreneurs? That's where the sixties went? Isn't life funny? As Charlie Brown once told his friend, "It depends on what the punch line turns out to be."

Friendship

A large part of this book has been about us and our emotions. So, I'd like to take one more shot at making sense of it here. One of the most common examples of how badly things can become botched, in the interplay of people and their feelings, is what happens when two people are together and one person is immersed in sadness. I tell you I'm sad. You feel my sadness, and it makes you feel bad. Maybe it also makes you feel that as long as I'm sad, I can't meet any of your needs.

So you feel alone even though we are together. You want me to stop feeling sad so you can start to feel better. You say something that is seemingly comforting, but I get the main point. You are telling me a way that I can think about what has just happened that supposedly will stop me from feeling sad about it. But that is really your disguised way of telling me you would prefer it if I didn't feel sad because my feeling this way bothers you. Now I'm even sadder, and I may be angry too.

You are communicating to me that you don't like my feelings, my insides. I've lost you too. I'm even more alone than I thought.

The variety of such clashes between my insides and your insides is infinite and may be what led one philosopher to say that hell is other people. Your needs and mine will never overlap completely, and in my attempts to make myself feel good, I may make you feel bad, and then you may make me feel bad for making you feel bad.

The magic moments are those times when someone else is in it with you. You know that they know how you feel, and your feeling that way is just great with them. Your happiness mirrors theirs, or they recognize your bad feeling and let you know you can have it as long as you need to and they will just be there anyway.

A great friendship can be built out of a few such moments. It can be maintained through periods of disappointment and even hatred by a sprinkling of them here and there.

How Analysts Became People

If I hadn't spent twenty years in small rooms talking with other people about their lives and mine, I would never have thought of this book, much less written it. So, I want to end it by saying something about the adulthood of psychotherapists, especially those therapists we refer to as psychoanalysts. Sometimes patients wonder about the process by which someone becomes an analyst. And enough books have been written about that process to constitute a separate genre in Western literature. Recently, however, the opposite question has been raised by a number of psychoanalysts, among them Jonathan Slavin of the Massachusetts Institute for Psychoanalysis and Karen Rosica of the Colorado Center for Psychoanalytic Studies—is it possible for a person, having become a psychoanalyst, to become a helpful therapist and perhaps even a person again?

Over the years many diatribes have been launched against

psychoanalysis by ex-patients who were not helped or were made to feel worse during a long analysis. There are, of course, people who hate a dentist they once saw or a lawyer who once represented them, but I have never seen an article in a major mainstream magazine arguing for the end of dentistry as a profession or telling people never to consult an attorney. I have seen such articles about psychoanalysis.

I believe they are all correct, yet I practice analysis anyway. If people didn't idealize their therapist at some time during treatment, they probably wouldn't be influenced enough to change. If, however, therapists idealize themselves and their theories, they will inevitably humiliate and enrage their patients. And analysts have probably shown as much of that tendency, if not more, than any other group of therapists.

What's been happening in psychoanalysis lately is reflected in a couple of papers written by the two people I mentioned earlier. Analysts are trying to figure out how to keep their theoretical and technical training from distancing them so much from the fundamental emotional experience of life that they cannot be fully present and open to new moments in their relationships with their patients. And it's working. There is a renewed interest among psychologists in this new brand of psychoanalysis.

This isn't a sales pitch for analysis. My point is to highlight the resistance to change among even those experts who help people change. It took a long time for many analysts to tolerate the emergence of this new perspective and the changes it implies in how they would work with patients and the kinds of competencies that would be required of them to be useful to a broad range of people. It was comforting to imagine that what being an analyst was about was becoming the captain of your own emotional vessel and then guiding other conflicted souls through the metaphorical rapids and passages of their lives.

And it was even more comforting to think that all you had to do was interpret and keep interpreting, and everyone would get better and be grateful and you'd be satisfied and well-off. It was comforting but unreal. It was the way we felt in the adolescence of psychoanalysis. Now we are growing up, and analysis looks messier. It's a place where we get drawn into other people's interpersonal dances and flounder around and then try to make sense of what is happening—from the inside—and finally get ourselves off that dance floor, hopefully, along with the patient. Then we do it again to a different tune. And we do it over and over until we find ourselves in some new relational routines—new for us and them. In the end we hope the people with whom we have done this work are not simply better informed about themselves but more competent at managing their emotions and their relationships.

That's how analysts have grown up, and it has been painful for many of us. The old way seemed so neat and certain and precise. But what Jon Slavin and Karen Rosica have been arguing, in some of the most elegant papers I have heard or read recently, is, as I've understood it, that growing up means in analysis what it means everywhere else in life—proceeding without absolute rules and definitive authority, tolerating confusion, and taking risks in the most uncertain arena of all, that of human relationships.

The basic tension in life, I have come to think, is between changing and not changing. It's a conflict that can be felt every day in every area of our life. It's a psychic war of the liberal and the conservative inside all of us—a war perpetuated by our desire to know that if and when we change, we are keeping all that works best and getting rid of only what doesn't, and so we won't regret it in the end.

But, as the old priest concluded in John Gardner's novel *Grendel*, "Things fade; alternatives exclude." An adulthood is a decision, and like all decisions, it costs you everything else—in this case the transcendent specialness of childhood and the unlimited possibility of adolescence, as well as all the other adulthoods you might have had. But as Humpty Dumpty told Alice, it's really too late for that now anyway.